365
Prayers
FOR
Catholic Schools and
Parish Youth Groups

INTERACTIVE ➜ SEASONAL ➜ TRADITIONAL

FILOMENA TASSI and **PETER TASSI**

D1319547

TWENTY-THIRD PUBLICATIONS

twentythirdpublications.com

TWENTY-THIRD PUBLICATIONS
1 Montauk Avenue, Suite 200, New London, CT 06320
(860) 437-3012 » (800) 321-0411 » www.twentythirdpublications.com

ISBN:978-1-62785-209-8
Library of Congress Catalog Card Number: 2016909028
Printed in the U.S.A.

CONTENTS

DEDICATION

We dedicate this book to the memory of our father,
Phil Tassi (1928-2006), a blacksmith and millwright
who dedicated his life to others, being the face of Jesus
to all who met him. His wisdom, profound views on life,
and infinite capacity to love and forgive inspired us all
to live out the gospel message.

• • •

ACKNOWLEDGMENTS

Thank you to Twenty-Third Publications for their faith
*in our work and for publishing this follow up to **500 Prayers***
***for Catholic Schools and Parish Youth Groups**.*
Their commitment to their mission informs and enlightens
their readers with a better understanding of church and God.
Thank you to the educators with whom we have worked,
and most of all, thank you to the youth, who are a blessing
to serve and work with.

Introduction

We hope you find this prayer book
a useful tool in your schools, parishes, youth
groups, and organizations. What better way to start
a day, an event, or a class than with a prayer? This book provides
a comprehensive, all-in-one prayer book covering traditional
prayers and practices, prayers for the liturgical seasons, saints'
feast days and celebrations, as well as a host of interactive prayers
covering a wide range of topics/themes relevant to young people.

The Traditional Prayers and Practices will not only serve as a
great review of our traditional prayers but will guide us in practices such as praying the Rosary and the Stations of the Cross.
Prayers for our Liturgical Seasons will not only provide a better
understanding of the liturgical calendar but will also promote
spiritual reflection during these most important times. Saints'
Days and Celebrations mark some of the days important to us all,
while each prayer highlights some of the great attributes of our
saints and provides encouragement to help us foster our personal
and spiritual growth.

Finally, the Interactive Prayers for Daily Life serve a dual
function. First, they lead us to pray on relevant topics important
to teenage life, encouraging the youth to find inspiration and
consolation through their faith and spiritual life. Second, they will
stimulate discussion on these topics through the use of reflection
questions that challenge us to think about the topic from a faith
perspective as well as from social and personal viewpoints. It is
our hope that these reflection questions will serve as a catalyst,

encouraging the youth to share and to discuss those issues that most concern them. We encourage the teachers/facilitators to add questions they believe will further stimulate discussion.

365 Prayers was not only written for Catholic schools, parish youth groups, and those leading group prayer. As well, it is an excellent guide and source for prayer and reflection in the life of any Catholic.

We hope that you find this prayer book a useful tool in helping you and your students grow in faith. We hope that it serves to strengthen your relationship with God as well as with his children. Finally, we hope this prayer book strengthens and inspires you to move forward every day in helping to build God's kingdom.

TRADITIONAL PRAYERS AND PRACTICES

Traditional Prayers

Act of Contrition

My God, I am sorry for my sins with all my heart. In choosing to do wrong and failing to do good, I have sinned against you whom I should love above all things. I firmly intend, with your help, to do penance, to sin no more, and to avoid whatever leads me to sin. Our Savior Jesus Christ suffered and died for us. In his name, my God, have mercy. [RITE OF PENANCE, NO. 45]

Act of Faith

O my God, I firmly believe that you are one God in three divine persons, Father, Son, and Holy Spirit. I believe that your divine Son became man and died for our sins, and that he will come to judge the living and the dead. I believe these and all the truths which the holy Catholic Church teaches, because you have revealed them who are eternal truth and wisdom, who can neither deceive nor be deceived. In this faith I intend to live and die. Amen.

Act of Hope

O Lord God, I hope by your grace for the pardon of all my sins and after life here to gain eternal happiness, because you have promised it who are infinitely powerful, faithful, kind, and merciful. In this hope I intend to live and die. Amen.

Act of Love

O Lord God, I love you above all things, and I love my neighbor for your sake, because you are the highest, infinite, and perfect good, worthy of all my love. In this love I intend to live and die. Amen.

Anima Christi

Soul of Christ, sanctify me. Body of Christ, save me. Blood of Christ, inebriate me. Water from the side of Christ, wash me. Passion of Christ, strengthen me. O good Jesus, hear me. Within your wounds conceal me. Do not permit me to be parted from you. From the evil foe protect me. At the hour of my death call me. And bid me come to you, to praise you with all your saints forever and ever. Amen.

Apostles' Creed

I believe in God, the Father almighty, Creator of heaven and earth, and in Jesus Christ, his only Son, our Lord, who was conceived by the Holy Spirit, born of the Virgin Mary; suffered under Pontius Pilate, was crucified, died and was buried; he descended into hell; on the third day he rose again from the dead; he ascended into heaven, and is seated at the right hand of God the Father almighty; from there he will come to judge the living and the dead. I believe in the Holy Spirit, the holy catholic Church, the communion of saints, the forgiveness of sins, the resurrection of the body, and life everlasting. Amen.

Confiteor *(traditional version)*

I confess to Almighty God, to blessed Mary ever virgin, to blessed Michael the archangel, to blessed John the Baptist, to the holy apostles Peter and Paul, and to all the saints that I have sinned exceedingly, in thought, word and deed, through my fault, through my fault, through my most grievous fault. Therefore I beseech blessed Mary, ever virgin, blessed Michael the archangel, blessed John the Baptist, the holy apostles Peter and Paul, all the Saints, and you, Father, to pray to the Lord our God for me.

Divine Praises

Blessed be God. Blessed be his holy name. Blessed be Jesus Christ, true God and true man. Blessed be the name of Jesus. Blessed be his most sacred heart. Blessed be his most precious blood. Blessed be Jesus in the most holy sacrament of the altar. Blessed be the great mother of God, Mary most holy. Blessed be her holy and immaculate conception. Blessed be her glorious assumption. Blessed be the name of Mary, virgin and mother. Blessed be St. Joseph, her most chaste spouse. Blessed be God in his angels and in his saints.

Glory Be

Glory be to the Father, and to the Son, and to the Holy Spirit, as it was in the beginning, is now, and ever shall be, world without end. Amen.

Grace Before Meals

Bless us, O Lord, and these your gifts, which we are about to receive from your bounty, through Christ our Lord. Amen.

Grace Before Meals

The eyes of all look to you, O Lord, to give them their food in due season. You open wide your hands and fill all things with your blessings, through Christ our Lord. Amen.

Grace After Meals

We give you thanks, Almighty God, for all thy gifts that we have received, through Christ our Lord. Amen.

Grace After Meals

For these and his many mercies, may the Lord's name be blessed, now and forever, through Christ Our Lord. Amen.

Grail Prayer

Lord Jesus, I give you my hands to do your work. I give you my feet to go your way. I give you my eyes to see as you do. I give you my tongue to speak your words. I give you my mind that you may think in me. Above all, I give you my heart that you may love in me your Father and all mankind. I give you my whole self that you may grow in me, so that it is you, Lord Jesus, who will live and work and pray in me. Amen.

Guardian Angel

Heavenly Father, Your infinite love for us has chosen a blessed angel in heaven and appointed him our guide during this earthly pilgrimage. Accept our thanks for so great a blessing. Grant that we may experience the assistance of our holy protector in all our necessities. And you, holy, loving angel and guide, watch over us with all the tenderness of your angelic heart. Keep us always on the way that leads to heaven, and cease not to pray for us until we have attained our final destination, eternal salvation. Amen.

Hail, Holy Queen

Hail, holy Queen, mother of mercy, our life, our sweetness, and our hope. To you we cry, poor banished children of Eve; to you we send up our sighs, mourning and weeping in this valley of tears. Turn, then, most gracious advocate, your eyes of mercy toward us; and after this, our exile, show unto us the blessed fruit of your womb, Jesus. O clement, O loving, O sweet Virgin Mary.

Hail Mary

Hail Mary, full of grace, the Lord is with you; blessed are you among women, and blessed is the fruit of your womb, Jesus. Holy Mary, Mother of God, pray for us sinners now and at the hour of our death. Amen.

Memorare

Remember, O most gracious virgin Mary, that never was it known that anyone who fled to your protection, implored your help, or sought your intercession, was left unaided. Inspired with this confidence, we fly unto you, O virgin our Mother. To you we come, before you we kneel, sinful and sorrowful. O Mother of the Word Incarnate, despise not our petitions, but in your mercy hear and answer them. Amen.

Morning Offering

O Jesus, through the Immaculate Heart of Mary, I offer you my prayers, works, joys, and sufferings of this day for all intentions of your Sacred Heart, in union with the Holy Sacrifice of the Mass throughout the world, for the salvation of souls, the reparation of sins, the reunion of all Christians, and in particular for the intentions of the Holy Father this month. Amen.

Nicene Creed

I believe in one God, the Father almighty, maker of heaven and earth, of all things visible and invisible. I believe in one Lord Jesus Christ, the Only Begotten Son of God, born of the Father before all ages. God from God, Light from Light, true God from true God, begotten, not made, consubstantial with the Father; through him all things were made. For us men and for our salvation he came down from heaven, and by the Holy Spirit was incarnate of the Virgin Mary, and became man. For our sake he was crucified under Pontius Pilate, he suffered death and was buried, and rose again on the third day in accordance with the Scriptures. He ascended into heaven and is seated at the right hand of the Father. He will come again in glory to judge the living and the dead and his kingdom will have no end. I believe in the Holy Spirit, the Lord, the giver of life, who proceeds from the Father and the Son, who with the Father and the Son is adored and glorified, who has spoken through the prophets. I believe in one, holy, catholic and apostolic Church. I confess one Baptism for the forgiveness of sins and I look forward to the resurrection of the dead and the life of the world to come. Amen.

Prayer Before a Crucifix

Look down upon me, good and gentle Jesus, while before your face I humbly kneel and, with burning soul, pray and beseech you to fix deep in my heart lively sentiments of faith, hope, and charity; true contrition for my sins, and a firm purpose of amendment. While I contemplate, with great love and tender pity, your five most precious wounds, pondering over them within me and calling to mind the words which David, your prophet, said to you, my Jesus: "They have pierced my hands and my feet, they have numbered all my bones."

Prayer to the Holy Spirit

Spirit of wisdom and understanding, enlighten our minds to perceive the mysteries of the universe in relation to eternity. Spirit of right judgment and courage, guide us and make us firm in our baptismal decision to follow Jesus' way of love. Spirit of knowledge and reverence, help us to see the lasting value of justice and mercy in our everyday dealings with one another. May we respect life as we work to solve problems of family and nation, economy and ecology. Spirit of God, spark our faith, hope, and love into new action each day. Fill our lives with wonder and awe in your presence, which penetrates all creation. Amen.

The Angelus

The Angel of the Lord declared unto Mary and she conceived of the Holy Spirit. Hail Mary... Behold the handmaid of the Lord, be it done unto me according to your Word. Hail Mary... And the Word was made flesh and dwelt among us. Hail Mary... Pray for us, O holy Mother of God, that we may be made worthy of the promises of Christ. Pour forth, we beseech You, O Lord, your grace into our hearts: that we, to whom the Incarnation of your Son was made known by the message of an Angel, may by his Passion and Cross be brought to the glory of his Resurrection. Through the same Christ Our Lord. Amen.

The Lord's Prayer

Our Father, who art in heaven, hallowed be thy name; thy kingdom come, thy will be done on earth as it is in heaven. Give us this day our daily bread, and forgive us our trespasses, as we forgive those who trespass against us; and lead us not into temptation, but deliver us from evil. Amen.

The Prayer for the Dead

God our Father, your power brings us to birth, your providence guides our lives, and by your command we return to dust. Lord, those who die still live in your presence; their lives change but do not end. I pray in hope for my family, relatives, and friends, and for all the dead known to you alone. In company with Christ, who died and now lives, may they rejoice in your kingdom, where all our tears are wiped away. Unite us together again in one family, to sing your praise forever and ever. Amen.

Traditional Practices

The Rosary

Through praying the Rosary we remember important events in the history of our salvation. There are twenty mysteries for which we give thanks. They are divided into the Joyful Mysteries, the Luminous Mysteries, the Sorrowful Mysteries, and the Glorious Mysteries. Our church recommends saying the Joyful Mysteries on Monday and Saturday and the Sundays of Advent, the Luminous on Thursday, the Sorrowful on Tuesday and Friday and the Sundays of Lent, and the Glorious on Wednesday and Sunday (except in Advent and Lent).

HOW TO PRAY THE ROSARY

- With the crucifix of the rosary, make the sign of the cross and say the Apostles' Creed.

- Say the Our Father on the first bead.

- Say three Hail Marys on the next three beads.

- Say the Glory Be.

- Announce the first Mystery and then say the Our Father.

- While fingering the next ten beads, say ten Hail Marys while meditating on the Mystery.

- Say the Glory Be.

- After the Rosary pray: "Hail Holy Queen, Mother of Mercy, our life, our sweetness and our hope. To you do we cry, poor banished children of Eve. To you do we send up our sighs, mourning and weeping in this valley of tears. Turn then, most gracious advocate, your eyes of mercy toward us, and after this exile show unto us the blessed fruit of thy womb, Jesus. O clement, O loving, O sweet Virgin Mary. Pray for us, O Holy Mother of God, that we may be made worthy of the promises of Christ.

THE MYSTERIES
The Joyful Mysteries

- The Annunciation: Mary learns that she has been chosen to be the mother of Jesus.

- The Visitation: Mary visits Elizabeth, who tells her that she will always be remembered.

- The Nativity: Jesus is born in a stable in Bethlehem.

- The Presentation: Mary and Joseph take infant Jesus to the Temple to present him to God.

- Finding Jesus in the Temple: Jesus is found in the Temple discussing faith with teachers.

The Luminous Mysteries

- The Baptism of Jesus in the River Jordan: God proclaims that Jesus is his beloved Son.

- The Wedding Feast at Cana: At Mary's request, Jesus performs his first miracle.

- The Proclamation of the Kingdom of God: Jesus calls all to service of the kingdom.

- The Transfiguration of Jesus: Jesus is revealed in glory to Peter, James, and John.

- The Institution of the Eucharist: Jesus offers his body and blood at the Last Supper.

The Sorrowful Mysteries

- The Agony in the Garden: Jesus prays in the Garden of Gethsemane on his final night.

- The Scourging at the Pillar: Jesus is lashed with whips.

- The Crowning with Thorns: Jesus is mocked and crowned with thorns.

- The Carrying of the Cross: Jesus carries the cross that will be used to crucify him.

- The Crucifixion: Jesus is nailed to the cross and dies.

The Glorious Mysteries

· The Resurrection: God the Father raises Jesus from the dead.

· The Ascension: Jesus returns to his Father in heaven.

· The Coming of the Holy Spirit: The Holy Spirit comes to bring new life to the disciples.

· The Assumption of Mary: After her death, Mary is taken body and soul into heaven.

· The Coronation of Mary: Mary is crowned as queen of heaven and earth.

The Stations of the Cross

The Stations of the Cross commemorate the passion of Christ, recalling the day of Jesus' crucifixion. The Stations of the Cross are also called the Way of Sorrows or, simply, the Path. The stations are most commonly done during Lent, especially on Good Friday, but may also be done any time one chooses.

OPENING PRAYER: Say the Act of Contrition

At the beginning of each station, announce the station and then say this prayer:

LEADER: We adore you, O Christ, and we praise you.

ALL: Because by your holy cross you have redeemed the world.

At the end of each station say an Our Father, a Hail Mary, and a Glory Be to the Father. Then pray this prayer:

LEADER: Jesus Christ crucified.

ALL: Have mercy on us.

LEADER: May the souls of the faithful departed,
through the mercy of God, rest in peace.

ALL: Amen.

FIRST STATION

Jesus is condemned to death

Jesus, you devoted your life to serving others, and yet when you stood before Pilate, there was nobody to help you. You stood alone. Lord, there are times in my life when I feel alone. I am committed to doing what I believe is right, and while others are preoccupied with what they are doing, I stand firm in my faith and love for you. Be with me, Lord, and give me the strength to endure these situations. May I always have the courage to do what I believe is right and to know that you are with me.

SECOND STATION

Jesus takes up his cross

Jesus, you accepted your cross and carried it to your death on Calvary. You knew it would not be easy and that you would endure great suffering, but you did it anyway. Lord, allow me to be patient when parents, friends, or teachers do not understand me; allow me to be generous when many others are only concerned with their own lives; give me courage to do what is right even though doing what is right may bring criticism and ridicule.

THIRD STATION
Jesus falls the first time

Jesus, the cross you carried was heavy, and you were tired and weak from the beatings you had taken. You fell, and even though nobody was there to help you and nobody seemed to care, you got up and carried on. Lord, there are times in my life when I feel tired and weak. It is as if I fall to my knees in failure. Help me to realize, Lord, that it is okay to fall, but what is most important is that I never quit—that I get back up and continue my journey.

FOURTH STATION
Jesus meets his mother

Jesus, you felt completely alone, and the people continued to yell and scream at you. As you felt it almost too much to bear, you saw your mother. Lord, open my eyes to the people who love me. Although they may not always be able to help me, I pray to see that they do love me and care for me, and if they could, they would do what needs to be done to rid me of my loneliness.

FIFTH STATION
Jesus is helped by Simon of Cyrene

Jesus, just as you thought you could go no farther, the soldiers told Simon to help you. Lord, as much as life can bring us pain, it can also bring us unexpected support. Sometimes when we least expect it and we think that all is lost, someone comes to our aid. We are grateful to those who are there to carry us on our journey, to bring us hope in our darkest times. And we pray, Lord, that we will always have the insight to see and the strength to help others who are in need of us.

SIXTH STATION

Veronica wipes Jesus' face with her veil

Jesus, Veronica came out of the crowd to wipe the blood and
sweat from your face. She truly cared for you. She was unable to
do much, but enough to let you know that she felt your suffering.
There will be times, Lord, when friends, teachers, or parents
cannot take away my suffering, but they are there to help me.
They wipe away my tears, offer a kind word, and are with me
through the difficult times. Their love will be a source of strength
for me.

SEVENTH STATION

Jesus falls the second time

Lord, your journey was long, difficult, and painful; you fell once
again. But in spite of exhaustion and suffering, you arose once
again and continued your journey. Lord, once again you teach
us that no matter how many times we fall, we must get up once
again. When we are tempted to feel total despair, help us to
know that you are with us. Give us the strength to persevere, to
overcome all the obstacles. In this way, Lord, you offer us the
opportunity for greatness.

EIGHTH STATION

Jesus speaks to the women of Jerusalem

Jesus, even though you were abandoned by friends, you mustered
up the strength and made time to talk to, encourage, and help the
women of Jerusalem. Lord, we pray that we never get so wrapped
up in our own lives that we lose sight of others. Grant us this great
capacity for love so that, even during the most difficult times, we
have the capacity to see the needs of others and the strength to
reach out and help them.

NINTH STATION

Jesus falls a third time

Jesus, your journey became almost unbearable. You fell for a third time beneath the weight of the cross. Yet you still managed to get up to finish the journey. Lord, I have fallen so many times in life. It seems as if I try my best and yet I continue to fail and sin. I just can't shed those weaknesses. Help me think of the cross you carried and realize that no matter how hard it gets, I can continue and I can make changes in my life.

TENTH STATION

Jesus is stripped of his garments

Jesus, you were whipped, tortured, mocked, and spat at. To further humiliate you, they stripped you of your clothes. They tried to strip you even of your pride, but you simply turned your eyes to heaven. Lord, it hurts to be criticized, gossiped about, or made fun of. When this happens to me, help me to turn my eyes to you and to trust in your loving presence. No matter how people treat me, they cannot take away my integrity and your love for me.

ELEVENTH STATION

Jesus is nailed to the cross

Jesus, large nails were hammered through your hands and feet. As the cross was lifted, you bled more, and you gasped for air as you hung from those nails. Lord, sometimes I feel ashamed for the things I have done and failed to do. Yet I know that in your most painful death, you show me your forgiveness and offer me redemption. When I reflect on your death, it brings me great sorrow but also gratitude for the freedom you have offered me.

TWELFTH STATION

Jesus dies on the cross

Jesus, in the midst of unbearable suffering and prior to breathing your last breath, you forgave those who crucified you and prayed for your mother and friends. Even in your death you thought of others rather than yourself. Lord, there are times I get so entangled in my own life I fail to see others. So often I am ruled by my own concerns and fail to see the suffering of others. Free me from self-centeredness so that I can be one with you and a caring person for others.

THIRTEENTH STATION

Jesus is taken down from the cross

Jesus, your suffering finally ended and your bloodied and beaten body was placed in the lap of your mother. Finally, it ended! You were then ready to join your Father. Lord, how many times I have taken others for granted! How many times I have not taken the opportunity to thank the people in my life! May I never take anyone for granted, and may I thank each and every person while they are alive for all the love and service they give to me.

FOURTEENTH STATION

Jesus is laid in the tomb

Jesus, they took you to your resting place and rolled a large stone over the entrance of your tomb. Although this was your final act of surrender, your tomb would soon be empty and you would show yourself alive to your disciples. I ask you, Lord, to give me your grace so that I may have the courage and strength to take up my cross and endure all things for your sake. I ask you that, like you, I too can be a beacon of light to others.

Holy Water

Holy water is water that has been blessed by a Catholic priest. Blessed water is a symbol of spiritual cleansing. When we bless ourselves with it by making the sign of the cross, it recalls our baptism and redirects our life to God. By recalling our baptism, we share in the passion, death, and resurrection of Jesus and begin anew.

Palms

In church or at home, the palms represent our homage and loyalty to Christ our King and Redeemer. They are a witness to our faith in Jesus as the messianic king and in his paschal victory. Blessed palms are also sacramentals, or sacred signs, preparing us to receive the sacraments or to sanctify situations. We celebrate with palms on Palm Sunday, the Sunday prior to Easter, the great celebration of Jesus' resurrection. This represents Jesus' entry into Jerusalem when the people placed palm branches in his path in recognition of his kingship. We sometimes make crosses out of palms. This reminds us to carry our cross patiently so that we may share in Christ's Easter glory.

Relics

Relics usually consist of the physical remains of a saint or the personal effects of the saint. Relics are not to be worshiped; only God is worshiped. Instead, we venerate and pray before the relics of the saints as a way to adore God.

Scapulars

The scapular was originally a monastic garment that hung over the shoulders, front and back of the wearer, and reaching to the knees. It is worn by monks to remind them of their commitment to live a Christian life. Devotional scapulars are much smaller pieces of cloth, a few inches in size, and bear religious images or text. These can be worn by any Christian.

PRAYERS FOR THE LITURGICAL YEAR

Advent Season

The Advent wreath is a Christian tradition symbolizing the passage of the four weeks of Advent. It is a circular candle holder that typically holds four candles. During the season of Advent one candle on the wreath is lit each Sunday, until all four candles are lit. There is the option to add a fifth candle, in the center of the wreath, to be lit on Christmas day. Each candle represents an aspect of the spiritual preparation for the celebration of the birth of our Lord Jesus Christ. Most Advent wreaths use three colors for the candles—purple, pink, and white.

FIRST SUNDAY AND WEEK OF ADVENT

Light first candle. Purple. Candle of hope.
We light the candle, representing hope. Hope, because God is faithful and will keep the promises made to us. God will send us the Messiah, the Son of God, as he promised. As we light the first candle, we ask God to fill our hearts and minds with hope.

God of hope, we enter your holy season of Advent giving thanks to you for the love you have for all of us. We begin to prepare for the celebration of the birth of our Lord and Savior, your Son,

Jesus. With the promise of your Son, we live with great hope and anticipation. Hope in the knowledge of the love you continue to give us. Hope in the knowledge that baby Jesus is coming into our lives and hearts to heal us and love us. We are a people of hope, and no matter how difficult times sometimes are, we know that your Son is coming and you continue to shower us with your love. Amen.

SECOND SUNDAY AND WEEK OF ADVENT
Light second candle. Purple. Candle of love.
Today we light the second candle, representing love. We prepare for the celebration of the birth of our Lord and hold within our hearts the abundance of love that our God brings to this world.

God of love, during this Advent season, when life is busy and excitement is in the air, we take time to think about the awesome gift of the birth of Jesus. We reflect on the great love you have for us that will be shown through your Son, Jesus. May the light of this candle reflect the light that resides within each of us, the love that we can bring to this world, and the healing we can offer those who are suffering. Amen.

THIRD SUNDAY AND WEEK OF ADVENT
Light third candle. Pink. Candle of joy
Today we light the third candle on our Advent wreath. The theme this week is joy. We are getting closer to celebrating the birth of our Lord and Savior and the great joy he brings to our lives.

God of joy, as we get closer to the celebration of the birth of your Son, we remain filled with joy. We know that life often presents us with challenges and that it is difficult to always be optimistic and cheerful. However, we know that you wish us to be a joy-filled people. Help us to focus on our blessings, to be appreciative of the many people who support us, and to be ever mindful of your constant presence. As we approach the celebration of Jesus' birth, may the peace and the joy of the season fill our hearts. Amen.

FOURTH SUNDAY AND WEEK OF ADVENT

Light Fourth Candle. Purple. Candle of peace.

Today we light the fourth candle on our Advent wreath. The theme this week is peace. Jesus is the Prince of Peace, and he brings healing to a broken world.

God of peace, in a troubled world where there is suffering and strife, conflict and war, we pray for peace. We also pray for inner peace, that our minds and bodies will be calm and at peace in the knowledge that you are about to come to us. Without inner peace, we know there can be no global peace, so we look to you, Lord, for your love and direction to calm ourselves and be instruments of peace in the world. Amen.

Christmas Season

Christmas Day. Nativity of Our Lord » *December 25*

LIGHT FIFTH CANDLE. WHITE.

JESUS IS THE SPOTLESS LAMB OF GOD.

Most generous God, my soul is filled with joy on this great day. Thank you for the gift of your Son, Jesus. With his birth we celebrate that the Messiah has come, that our Savior has been born, that the world is filled with hope, love, joy, and peace. The wise men knew that, at the moment of your Son's birth, it would be the dawn of a new age. They knew that the world would be changed. They knew that the day would come when baby Jesus would grow into a man and begin a ministry that would free us from the oppression of sin and offer us a whole new way of living. Amen.

Saint Stephen » *December 26*

Dear Lord, Stephen, your first martyr, was an example and inspiration to your early church, just as he is for us today. We pray for the gift of speech so that we may be a powerful voice for the poor, just as Saint Stephen was. We pray for the gift of courage so that we can stand up for the rights of others and do what is righteous, just as Saint Stephen did. We pray for the gift of conviction so that we will not waver in doing your will and stand up against injustice, just as Saint Stephen did. Amen.

Saint John the Evangelist » *December 27*

Dear God, your apostle and humble servant John, blessed with long life, served you, building your church in Jerusalem and writing down the Good News you brought to the world. We pray, Lord, that we, along with all our loved ones, will be blessed with health, peace, and a fulfilling life. We pray that, like John, all that we write, speak, and do will spread the Good News of your salvation. Amen.

Holy Innocents » *December 28*

Dear God, in fear that baby Jesus would become a ruler, King Herod had all male children under the age of two massacred in Bethlehem. Your Son, Jesus, escaped this genocide. We pray, Lord, that good will always triumph over evil. In spite of the evil in the world, we pray that we will continue to be faithful to you, devoted to the message of love, and determined to live the virtuous life, in the knowledge that good *will* triumph over evil. Amen.

Holy Family » *Sunday Between Christmas and New Year's Day*
Dear God, Mary, Joseph, and Jesus serve as a model for all families: they were faithful to your call, obedient to your will, and selflessly giving to each other. We are blessed with our own families. Help us to follow the example of the Holy Family by showing our own families devotion and love. Amen.

Mary, Mother of God » *January 1*
Dear Lord, we give thanks to you for the gift of Mary. Obedient to your will, determined to serve you and humanity, she played a critical role in salvation by giving birth to your Son, the Prince of Peace. We pray to find the wisdom and courage to be obedient to your will and play a part in the salvation you offer to all. May our every word and action make us instruments of love and peace. Amen.

Epiphany of the Lord
Dear Jesus, today we celebrate the feast of the Epiphany. We celebrate your infancy, when you were made known to the world as the Messiah and Savior. It is the gift of your life that transformed our world. Because of you we can grow into a people with greater love in our hearts, a greater ability to forgive, and a greater willingness to live in hope for your kingdom. Thank you, Lord, for the gift of yourself to us. Amen.

Baptism of the Lord
Dear Jesus, today, we celebrate your baptism in the Jordan River, when you were anointed by the Holy Spirit and then began

your public ministry. On this day, we are reminded of our own baptism, when we were anointed to share in your life, death, and resurrection. We pray that as a people anointed by the Holy Spirit we can use the gifts given to us to minister to this world. May we, through the gifts of the Holy Spirit, attend to the needs of all people. Amen.

Lenten Season

During these forty days of Lent, we are called to make some sacrifice or do something positive for others. Whatever we choose to do, we want it to be a sign of our love for God. Lent is a time of sacrifice but also a time of joy and hope. We are reminded of Jesus' suffering and the love he has for us. We cleanse and purify ourselves so that we can demonstrate this love to others.

Ash Wednesday

Most humble Lord, we need you in our lives. As we travel through Lent, we are reminded of our need for forgiveness and redemption. As much as we live to serve others, we sometimes feel guilty for being selfish, judgmental, and arrogant. We know that you are with us. It is our prayer that during Lent we will see clearly the life you call us to live. May we experience your forgiveness and love each day, making us better servants in our work to build your kingdom of love. The ashes placed on our foreheads are a reminder of the humility to which we are called. We remember that we are in need of your love and forgiveness. We pray to see and respond to the suffering of others, recognizing that we are all one human family. Amen.

First Week of Lent

Lord, although our intentions may be pure, we often fall to temptation and sin. We know that you love us. May your love sustain us, helping us to correct our wrongs, to get up when we have fallen, and to find strength in our weaknesses and victory in our failings. Amen.

Second Week of Lent

Lord, keep us humble so that we may not fall into the temptation to judge others. Bless us with humility so that we may never place ourselves above others. We pray to be less occupied with our own desires and more passionate about the needs of others. Amen.

Third Week of Lent

Lord, grant us the gifts of wisdom and prudence. With these virtues, we will always make decisions that are good for our mental and physical well-being. With wisdom and prudence, we will make healthy choices that will best serve the growth of our minds and bodies, living lives that exemplifies the greatness we have within. Amen.

Fourth Week of Lent

Dear Jesus, as we approach the Easter season and the experience of your passion, death, and resurrection, we feel grief as well as peace. We feel grief knowing the suffering and death you endured for our sake. We feel peace in the knowledge that you offer us a life filled with love and hope. We are comforted to know that you are always with us, loving us and embracing us in spite of our failures. Thank you, Lord. Amen.

Fifth Week of Lent

Forgiving Jesus, we feel great comfort as we come closer to Easter. We are comforted in knowing that you have come to forgive us our sins, that you suffered and died for us, and that you offer us resurrection and eternal life. We are honored to be called your disciples. We have great courage in knowing that we are Christians and can live our lives according to the path you set for us. We walk with you as you walk with us. Amen.

Palm Sunday

Dear Jesus, today we celebrate your triumphant entry into Jerusalem. Although the people hailed you as king and savior, you remained humble and focused on your mission. We pray that during this Holy Week we may recognize our own wonder and beauty and at the same time remain humble. May we spend this week preparing for your death and resurrection with a spirit of service to others and an open heart to all those in need. Amen.

Easter Triduum

Holy Thursday Evening to Easter Sunday Evening

As we enter this **Easter Tridium,** we pray for an understanding of the sacrifice in the passion, and the joy in the resurrection.

Suffering Jesus, we pray that the holiness of these three days may be with us. May your love and sacrifice become a part of who we are and what we do. We pray that, as you bore your suffering, we can bear our suffering. We pray that, as you died for our sins, we can die to our sins. We pray for the strength to overcome our obstacles and live the life you call us to. We pray that, as your resurrection offers us eternal life, we can live each day with hope. Amen.

Holy Thursday

Servant Jesus, at the Last Supper, you got on your knees, wrapped an apron around yourself, and washed the feet of your disciples. It was an act of service and unconditional love. On this sacred day, we are surrounded by signs, symbols, and images emphasizing the value of service. We pray that our own desires and needs never overshadow the dignity and integrity of those around us. May we follow your example at the Last Supper and learn to be true servants for others. Amen.

Good Friday

Crucified Jesus, on this day you suffered and died for us. Your sacrifice and great act of love offered us forgiveness and hope. May we also be a source of forgiveness and hope to others. May we have the capacity to forgive others who have hurt us, to accept those who have been rejected, and to offer hope to those in our community who are suffering. Amen.

Saturday Easter Vigil

Jesus, your resurrection gives us hope in eternal life as well as for living each and every day knowing that you are with us and that, no matter the situation, tomorrow brings the promise of a better day. We live with the virtue of patience, awaiting the gift of resurrection. We live each and every day with patience as we work and wait for the gifts life offers us. Amen.

Easter Sunday

Resurrected Jesus, today we celebrate your resurrection with great joy. You call us to live a life of joy and hope, and you offer us this life through your teachings and your resurrection. Even during difficult times, we not only live in hope, but we also live with great joy, viewing each and every day as a gift. There is no greater gift than to embrace life and all the beauty it offers. Amen.

Pentecost

Dear God, on this special day, you send us your Holy Spirit and the gifts the Holy Spirit offers: wisdom, understanding, counsel, knowledge, fortitude, piety, and fear of the Lord. These gifts help us to live out your message of love and life. These gifts, given to all of us in different degrees, help us to actualize our own greatness and to be an example to the world. Amen.

SAINTS AND CELEBRATIONS

Saint Teresa of Calcutta » *September 5*

Dear Lord, your humble servant Mother Teresa left her home at eighteen years of age to become a sister and a missionary. She heard your call and responded with courage and fortitude. Mother Teresa taught us to do all things, even the small things, with great love. We pray to always be open to your call and to have the courage to be humble servants. Give us the fortitude to build your kingdom through service to others, particularly children. Amen.

Birth of Mary » *September 8*

Generous Father, we are grateful for the gift of Mary, the mother of your Son, Jesus. This humble servant of yours, the daughter of Anne and Joachim, brought hope and the dawn of a new world. She serves as an inspiration and source of hope to all of us. Our lives are richer because of her humility, her wisdom, and her unconditional love. We pray that, like Mary, we may remain obedient to your will, bear our suffering with hope, and become a source of light to this world. Amen.

Holy Name of Mary » *September 12*

Dear Mary, for centuries we have prayed for your intercession. Over and over again, you respond and offer us protection and direction. You hear our prayers and act on our behalf. We thank you for all that you have given us. We continue to pray to our Lord through you. We ask that you continue to offer us love when we fail, hope when there is darkness, and guidance when we are lost. Amen.

Triumph of the Cross » *September 14*

Dear Jesus, everyone suffers to some degree. We may suffer from loss of loved ones or friendships, from falling short of expectations, from loneliness or stress. No matter the source of our suffering, we know that there is victory. Just as there was victory in your cross, our own suffering can make us stronger and better people. Our suffering can bring us to a place in life where we excel beyond our expectations and appreciate the wonder and beauty of ourselves and others. Amen.

Saint Matthew » *September 21*

Dear Lord, we pray for the gifts of writing and speaking that you gave to your apostle Mathew. You taught us, through your ministry, the power of kind and gentle words. When we speak or write words of kindness and gentleness to others, we win friendships and change people's lives. Kind words can alleviate the suffering of others and breathe hope into their lives. May every word we speak and write be words that empower others and bring joy to their lives. Amen.

Saint Vincent de Paul » *September 27*

Generous God, St. Vincent sold what he had and dedicated his life to serving the poor. We pray to be more like St. Vincent: compassionate, humble, and generous. May we see all people as our brothers and sisters and take every opportunity to help those in need by feeding the hungry, giving care to the sick, and offering comfort to those who suffer. Amen.

Saints Michael, Gabriel & Raphael
 » *September 29 (USA) or October 2 (Canada)*

Father, we pray to your saints Michael, Gabriel, and Raphael to protect us from all that deters us from our mission to build your kingdom on earth. May they safeguard us from harmful influences, steer us away from the temptation to hurt others out of concern for our own self-interest, help us overcome the fears and insecurities that prevent us from recognizing and embracing our own gifts, and guide us toward becoming an instrument of change in the world. Amen.

Saint Thérèse of Lisieux » *October 1*

Dear God, we thank you for the gift of Saint Thérèse, "The Little Flower of Jesus." She taught us how we might find great peace and joy in living a simple life of service. She often said, "My way is all confidence and love." May our way be simple but filled with confidence and love. Help us to know the infinite value in doing simple tasks of love for others. Amen.

Saint Francis of Assisi » *October 4*

Dear Lord, Saint Francis gave up all his wealth and spent his life serving the poor and living as one with nature and all its creatures. He saw your beauty in every aspect of creation.

Lord, you make it clear in your ministry that all of us have a responsibility to care for nature and serve the poor and the outcasts. Give to us the generosity of heart and the courage to live our lives like St. Francis. Amen.

Our Lady of the Rosary *» October 7*

Dear Mary, the Rosary has been a great source of strength and spiritual enlightenment for much of Christian history. When we reflect on the Joyful Mysteries, we thank God for the gift of his Son. The Sorrowful Mysteries remind us of the suffering he endured for us. The Glorious Mysteries offer hope in the promise of the resurrection and life with you in heaven. The Luminous Mysteries offer us the possibility of God's kingdom here on earth. Amen.

Blessed Cardinal Newman *» October 9*

Dear Lord, Cardinal Newman worked endlessly to promote the value of Catholic education. Education plays a critical role in our faith development. Knowledge is power, and we pray that we will use the power we acquire through education to play our important part in building a better world. We pray that we will be your instrument in establishing your kingdom on earth. Amen.

Saint Teresa of Ávila *» October 15*

Dear Lord, your humble servant Saint Teresa of Ávila was a great nun, mystic, theologian, and writer. Lord, you have given gifts to each of us. We pray for self-discipline to work hard so that, like Saint Teresa, we can share our gifts with the world. May we overcome doubt, free ourselves from low self-esteem, find the courage to act, and have the wisdom to do what is right. We desire to exercise our gifts and, in so doing, create a world of love and peace. Amen.

Saint Marguerite d'Youville » *October 16*

God of hope, Saint Marguerite grew up in desperate poverty, was in an abusive marriage, and lost four of her six children. Even so, she did not give up. Following the death of her husband, she dedicated her life to the poor. In spite of many obstacles and even ridicule, she served thousands of impoverished people and orphaned children. Lord, give us the fortitude and endurance of Saint Marguerite. No matter how many obstacles we endure, we pray that we never lose sight of your tender love. May we continue to do good so that our life of love and service leaves no room for bitterness, anger, or negativity. Amen.

World Food Day » *October 16*

Dear Jesus, we give you thanks for the abundance of food and resources with which we have been blessed. Instill in us the willingness to sacrifice and give of ourselves so that others who are without the basic necessities of life may simply live. Millions of children die every year from malnutrition. Millions more do not develop properly because of a lack of food. We strive to be an example of your teaching, Jesus, to go out and feed the hungry. Give us the knowledge and the courage to be the voice of the poor, challenging our world leaders to make food supply and distribution their number one priority. Amen.

Saint Luke » *October 18*

Dear Jesus, Saint Luke told us your story through his gospel and the Acts of the Apostles. As a physician, historian, and writer, he made known to us your love for all people and the early history of your church. We pray that, like Saint Luke, we can spread your message of love to the world, your message that there is no room

for discrimination or judging others, that we are all equal and
of infinite worth, that there is no Jew or Gentile, black or white,
male or female, master or slave. We are all one, all worthy of
infinite love. Amen.

Saint Margaret Mary Alacoque *» October 16 (USA) 20 (Canada)*
Ever-present God, Saint Margaret Mary was initially rebuked by
her own church when she claimed that she had visions of your Son,
Jesus, and Mother Mary. But she did not waver; and because of her
efforts we celebrate the devotion to the Sacred Heart of Jesus. Saint
Margaret Mary helps us to see the great love Jesus had for us. God,
we are sometimes tempted to believe you have abandoned us during
difficult times. At the same time, we are tempted to turn away from
you when all is well and we believe we do not need you. We pray
that we always remain focused and clear minded, knowing that it
is your divine love that will sustain us and be a constant source of
inner joy. Amen.

Saint John Paul II *» October 22*
God of unity and harmony, Saint John Paul inspired us in his work
to bring together Jews, Christians, and Muslims. We pray that our
words and works are always for the unification of people, bringing
all people together as one human family. There always seems to
be too much fighting and war in the world. Even in our own circle
of family and friends, there is too much time spent disagreeing
and fighting with each other. We pray to be strong instruments of
unity, creating the one human family that you call us to be. Amen.

Halloween, "All Hallows Eve" *» October 31*
Dear God, we give you thanks for all harvests that feed our bodies
and souls. We give thanks for this special holiday, Halloween, and

all the anticipation and excitement it brings. We look forward
to wearing costumes, visiting neighbors, gathering candy, and
sharing some laughs with our friends. We pray that on this
evening, the night before All Saints Day, we will be kept safe and
joyful through the watchful eye of our saints. Amen.

All Saints Day » *November 1*

Dear God, today we give you thanks for all our saints. They have
provided us with a wonderful living witness to your love. They
have faithfully followed you and in so doing touched the lives of
so many here on earth. Lord, help us to follow the example of our
saints. May we be granted the faith and discipline to follow in
their footsteps. Amen.

All Souls Day » *November 2*

Dear God, today we remember our relatives and friends who have
died. We miss them dearly and wish that they were here with us.
Help us to get through our sorrow. Our grieving is a sign of our
love for them. We know that we were blessed with these people in
our lives, and that they continue to live on in us. God, may we be
comforted today in knowing that our loved ones are at peace, in
your embrace, and that one day we will see them again. Amen.

Saint Martin of Tours » *November 11*

God of peace, your humble servant Saint Martin was a Roman
soldier but refused to enter battle with a weapon and draw blood.
Instead, he devoted himself to nonviolence. Even as a soldier
he found ways to live like a monk, ministering to and feeding
his servants, being generous with the poor, and living as a poor
person. God, we pray that no matter what we choose to do in life,
we can find ways to be faithful to your message and live the life

you call us to. No matter what career we choose, we can find ways to serve you. Amen.

Veterans Day *(USA)* Remembrance Day *(Canada)*
» November 11

Dear Lord, we remember today all those who fought for peace and justice. No words can fully express the appreciation we have for all those who have made sacrifices and continue to make sacrifices. Bless them, Lord! Many gave their lives to thwart the cruelty and evil of dictators and to establish equality, freedom, and peace. For those who have died, we pray that they be with you in peace and joy, and that their families find comfort and peace. Amen.

Presentation of Mary *» November 21*

Dear Jesus, when your mother's parents, Saints Joachim and Anne, gave birth to Mary, they brought her to the temple to give thanks and to consecrate her to your Father in heaven. Like Saints Joachim and Anne, we give thanks to you and to your Father for the gift of salvation. Your life, your message, your death and resurrection are the ultimate gift to us. You free us from the guilt of our sins and show us the way to living with hope and joy. We consecrate our lives to you, promising to live out the life of love you call us to. Amen.

Thanksgiving

Heavenly Father, Thanksgiving is a wonderful time of year. We take time to truly appreciate what we have. Today, we give thanks to you for all our blessings. In his second letter to the Corinthians, Saint Paul says, "And God is able to provide you with every blessing in abundance, so that by always having enough of everything you may share abundantly in every good work." It is sometimes tempting to get caught up in the negativity and the woes of our lives. When we see that we are blessed with infinite gifts, we come to better appreciate nature, family, friends, talents, education, opportunities, and a God who loves us. Thank you, Lord, for all our gifts. Amen.

ChristL the King » *last Sunday of the liturgical year*

King of Kings, we pray that all world leaders lead with humility and recognize that they are in their positions to serve you and the people of their nations. We pray that they lead with wisdom, caring for the weakest members of their societies. We pray that they emulate you, being leaders of forgiveness, love, and peace. Amen.

Saint Francis Xavier » *December 3*

God of truth and justice, Saint Francis traveled the world spreading the Good News against great obstacles. He had a passion and zeal for telling people about the love and joy you offer. You call us to be a voice for truth and justice. We pray that we will have the courage to be that voice. We ask that you give us comfort when we are troubled, strength when we are weak, and courage when we are frightened. Grant us the passion and zeal of Saint Francis. With you at our side, we will be steadfast and bring your light of love and joy to the lives of others. Amen.

Immaculate Conception of Mary » *December 8*

Heavenly Father, your precious daughter Mary was conceived free of original sin. Although this gift was reserved for the precious mother of your Son, Jesus, we know that all of us are conceived in your image of beauty, love, and wisdom. You bring each of us into the world for a special purpose, giving to each of us unique gifts. We pray that we can live out our lives, as Mary did, fulfilling our gifts and bringing to the world everything we have to offer, for the glory of you and all your children. Amen.

Saint Basil the Great *» January 2*

Dear Lord, the importance of education is illustrated by the life of Saint Basil the Great. He used his great knowledge to write and to shape the direction of the church and monastic life. We pray that we will be dedicated to our studies and make every effort to acquire the schooling and knowledge we need to accomplish great things with our lives. We have the confidence of knowing that our education will make us rich in knowledge and free us from ignorance. Amen.

Holy Name of Jesus *» January 3*

Dear Jesus, when we pray in your name, we are reminded of your sacrifice for us and all the blessings you bestow upon us. When we call out to you, Jesus, you hear our prayer. When we seek your comfort, you find us and walk with us. Your name is all powerful. As Saint Paul reminds us in his letter to the Philippians, "at the name of Jesus every knee should bend, in heaven and on earth and under the earth." Amen.

Saint Elizabeth Ann Seton *» January 4*

Dear Lord, Saint Elizabeth is an inspiration to us. As a mother and a widow, she accomplished great things in her life. We pray for the vision that Elizabeth had, leading to the establishment of the first Catholic school in America as well as the first congregation of religious sisters there, the Sisters of Charity. Lord, we pray for the gift of prudence and perseverance, for self-confidence and courage, for compassion and kindness. With these virtues, Lord, we make our vision for a better world a reality. Amen.

Saint John Neumann » *January 5*

Dear God, your humble servant Saint John Neumann established the first diocesan system of Catholic schools in America. We give thanks for the gift of Catholic education. We promise to honor Saint John's undying devotion to the education of young people by being faithful to our studies and valuing the great contribution of our educators. May we never take for granted the gifts of knowledge and education and how each one prepares us for a career that best fulfills our calling. Amen.

Saint Anthony the Abbot » *January 17*

Dear Lord, Saint Anthony heard your call to give away all his material wealth and live the life of a monk. He had great courage, never doubting or fearing the life you asked him to live. We ask for that courage so that we will not fear or have any doubt about the life you call us to live. You have a special mission for each of us, Lord, and we respond in confidence, knowing that the life of love you desire us to live will bring us true joy. Amen.

Saint Agnes » January 21

Dear Lord, today we remember Saint Agnes, who gave her life as a martyr at the age of thirteen. She was a beautiful young girl. Because she would not marry a rich man, choosing instead to dedicate her life to you, she was put to death. Lord, we pray for the courage to follow our conscience and do what is right. May we always respond to your call, even though we may be ridiculed and suffer because of it. Amen.

Conversion of Saint Paul *» January 25*

Forgiving God, Saint Paul persecuted and killed Christians, but after being visited by you on his trip to Damascus, he changed his ways and became your greatest disciple. He is an example to us of your presence in our lives. Lord, we thank you for your mercy, for your forgiveness; for freeing us from the guilt we feel when we have sinned; for the redemption that you offer all your people. We thank you for being ever present in our lives, transforming us, as you did Saint Paul, to be great people. Amen.

Saint Thomas Aquinas *» January 28*

Dear God, Saint Thomas Aquinas is considered one of the greatest minds of the last one thousand years. After writing many books and shaping history, he claimed that he knew little and it all meant nothing in light of your infinite wisdom. He is an example of the greatest of virtues, the virtue of humility. We thank you, Lord, for calling each and every one of us to do great things. At the same time, we pray for the gift of humility, never boasting about ourselves or considering ourselves better than our brothers and sisters. Amen.

Saint John Bosco *» January 31*

God of love and life, your humble servant Saint John Bosco went out into the streets to take in orphans, to educate the street children, and to reform delinquent teenagers. When society gave up on these people, he would not. We pray that we have the heart to love, the mind to understand, and the eyes to see that no person is above or beneath us. We are all equal. We are all deserving of your infinite love. We pray that we will see, as Saint John Bosco did, the greatness in each person, especially those cast aside by society. Amen.

Saint Brigid » *February 1*

Dear Lord, Saint Brigid accomplished so much in her life, demonstrating boundless charity for those in distress, establishing several monasteries and schools and having many miracles attributed to her. We learn from Saint Brigid that one is able to do many great things in a short lifetime. We pray for the deep spirituality, the self-discipline, and the kind of attitude that Saint Brigid had. Believing in ourselves and having faith in you makes all things possible. Amen.

Presentation of our Lord » *February 2*

Dear God, as required by Jewish law, Mary presented her son, Jesus, in the Temple forty days after his birth. Simeon immediately recognized the greatness in the child and prophesied that the redemption of the world will come from him. We pray to you, God, that we have the insight and prophecy of Simeon, that we can recognize Jesus in our own lives and in the lives of others, and that we too will see and experience his redemptive power through the love and forgiveness he offered the world. Amen.

Saint Blaise » *February 3*

Healing God, as a doctor, Saint Blaise was as concerned with healing the soul as he was the body. Numerous miracles are attributed to his healing of the sick. Lord, you created us spiritual beings, and we pray for health and wholeness, for our mind, body, and soul. Sometimes, we place too much emphasis on our physical bodies, concerned solely about how we look, while neglecting to care for our minds, hearts, and souls. Help us to live a life that develops and heals our entire being so that we can be truly healthy. Amen.

World Day of Prayer for the Sick » *February 11*

Comforting God, you came to this world through your Son, Jesus, to care for and heal those who suffer. We pray for all those throughout the world who suffer because of hunger, illness, loneliness, and despair. We pray that we will be healing agents in their lives, offering them gentleness and kindness. We pray that we can do as you did and offer them the depth of love and acceptance that they need. Amen.

Our Lady of Lourdes » *February 11*

Dear Mary, you have appeared to many people over the centuries. Today we celebrate your apparitions, especially to Saint Bernadette at Lourdes in France. Through your apparitions you have inspired, healed, and transformed the lives of millions of people. We continue to pray to our Lord through you, that you will continue to be a source of light, comfort, and hope to all God's people. Just as you loved your Son, Jesus, we find comfort in knowing that you love us. Amen.

Valentine's Day » *February 14*

Dear Lord, we ask you to bless our special relationships. On this Valentine's Day, we not only celebrate the romantic love that exists between couples, we also celebrate the special love that exists between us and our family and friends. We give you thanks on this day for all those in our life whom we truly love. It is a great gift to have people in our lives who care for us, love us, provide for us, and do all they can to support and guide us. May we continue to be blessed with loving people who will always be there for us. Amen.

Saint David » *March 1*

Dear Lord, throughout his life, Saint David established many monasteries and churches and demonstrated that true peace and happiness come from service to you. Saint David inspires us not to be materialistic and helps us to see that happiness does not come through acquiring material things or obtaining power. It does not come from seeking pleasures of the body. Happiness comes from living a disciplined life and a life of love and service to others. Amen.

Saint Patrick » *March 17*

Dear Lord, Saint Patrick, patron saint of Ireland, teaches us to never give up. In spite of being a childhood slave, and in spite of the many obstacles he later encountered as a priest, Saint Patrick would not waver from his beliefs and his mission. Lord, sometimes we are overwhelmed by the obstacles in our lives. We grow tired and weak. It is at these moments that we pray for your help. We cannot walk this journey alone; but through your help we can conquer all things. Amen.

Saint Joseph, Husband of Mary » *March 19*

Dear Lord, Saint Joseph used his gift for carpentry to provide Mary and Jesus with comfort and security. He dedicated his life to serving you through his family. We pray for this same dedication and commitment to serving others. We all have a special gift, and you call all of us to serve you through our gifts—the gift of writing or speaking, the gift of organizing or leadership, the gift of athletics or academics, the gift of compassion or the ability to listen and care for others. There are an infinite number of gifts, but no matter what our gift is, we pray that we use them to best serve you. Amen.

The Annunciation » *March 25*

Dear God, the Annunciation commemorates the time when the angel Gabriel told Mary that she would conceive Jesus by the Holy Spirit. This must have come as quite a shock to Mary, as she was unmarried and a virgin. However, she was obedient and responsive to your call. Mary never hesitated to say "yes" to God's invitation. Lord, you call all of us, and we pray that we too will be able to overcome any fears and have the courage that Mary had. We pray that we too will respond to do your work without hesitation and with joy in our hearts. Amen.

Saint Bernadette » *April 16*

Dear Jesus, after Saint Bernadette's visions of your mother at Lourdes, she encouraged all of us to be prayerful and to practice penance. We pray that our life will be one of prayer. May we reflect your beauty and love in every word we speak and every deed we do. Help us to avoid gossip, negative speaking, and actions that hurt the feelings or lives of others. We also pray in penance, realizing that we are not perfect, knowing that if we are truly sorry, we will be forgiven and begin each day anew. Amen.

Saint Kateri Tekakwitha » *April 17*

Dear Lord, Saint Kateri, one of your many Native American followers, was a testimony to the great joy and fulfillment found in living a life of virtue. We pray to live a life of virtue, to acquire the virtues of compassion, empathy, humility, courage, determination, truthfulness, peacefulness, and justice. We seek this life of virtue because through this we will experience the treasures of peace and joy that you offer. Amen.

Saint Mark » *April 25*

Dear Jesus, we give thanks for Saint Mark and the gospel he wrote, telling us of your life. We give thanks for all the sacred Scriptures, from the Book of Genesis to the Book of Revelation. They tell us the story of salvation. The Holy Scriptures not only inform your people but have changed the world, bringing people to you and creating your kingdom here on earth. We pray that, throughout our lives, your words always serve as our guide, showing us how to behave, the attitude we should have, and the work we should do to create your kingdom here on earth. Amen.

Saint Catherine of Siena » *April 29*

Dear Lord, your humble servant Saint Catherine lived a virtuous life, totally devoted to serving you and your church. We pray that we too will acquire the virtues of enthusiasm, diligence, perseverance, and patience. Like Saint Catherine, may we accomplish great things through a life of virtue and devotion to you. Amen.

Saint Joseph the Worker » *May 1*

Dear St. Joseph, foster father to Jesus and carpenter, you are the patron saint of workers. We ask you to watch over us and guide us in the work we do inside and outside our school community. Just as you worked to give a comfortable life to Mary and Jesus, we pray that our work at home will bring comfort to our family. Just as you worked as a carpenter to provide for your community, we pray that our work at school and community, through clubs and extracurricular activities, will help build a stronger community. Amen.

Ascension of the Lord » *40 days after Easter Sunday*

Dear Jesus, your ascension into heaven, as witnessed by your apostles, is our greatest light of hope. For all of us, to be one with you is the ultimate source of joy. We live our lives on earth working to be a source of love and joy, to be a beacon of light for others, and to be one with you. In our thoughts, in our words, and in our actions, we are one with you. In this oneness with you, our lives are filled with joy. Thank you, Jesus. Amen.

Saint Joan of Arc » *May 30*

Dear Lord, Saint Joan of Arc attended Mass and went to confession regularly so that her mind was clear and open to your call. We pray for the same toughness, diligence, and perseverance. You call all of us, Lord, to do difficult tasks. Sometimes we will suffer the criticisms of others. But we pray for the virtues and the gift of the Holy Spirit so that we will have the courage to do what we believe is right. Amen.

Visitation of Mary » *May 31*

Dear Jesus, your mother, Mary, while pregnant with you, made the long journey to visit her cousin Elizabeth, who was pregnant with John. During those times when we are burdened and even overwhelmed, give us the strength to reach out to others who may need our help. Throughout these acts of charity, you are with us and will lighten our load. You are always with us, and we have nothing to fear. Amen.

Corpus Christi

Dear Jesus, thank you for the gift of your Body and Blood in the Eucharist. We are spiritually enriched through having received your Body and Blood. We are reminded of your life, passion, death, and resurrection whenever we receive your Eucharist. May it strengthen us when we walk a difficult path and enlighten us when we are lost. Amen.

Saint Anthony of Padua » *June 13*

Most gracious God, you gave Saint Anthony the ability to preach. The spoken word is powerful and inspiring, empowering others to greatness. We pray that you continue to bless our preachers, sending them the Holy Spirit so they can continue to spread your word and bring us all closer to you. We also pray that, in our own way, our words will be powerful messages of your love, forgiveness, and joy. Amen.

Saint Thomas More » *June 22*

Dear God, what a great man we see when we look at Saint Thomas More. He served you throughout his life as a lawyer, philosopher, statesman, and as chancellor of England. We admire him most of all for his courage to risk his life by standing up to King Henry VIII. His stand cost him his life. It is our prayer and hope that we have the courage of Saint Thomas More to always follow what our conscience believes to be right, even in the face of rejection and persecution. Amen.

Sacred Heart of Jesus

Dear Jesus, your physical heart is a reminder of your divine love for humanity. At times, we do not feel worthy of love. We make mistakes, we fail, and we sin. When these things happen, we feel insecure and vulnerable, unworthy of love. Help us to see, Lord Jesus, that we are precious, of infinite value, and worthy of your love and mercy. Amen.

Immaculate Heart of Mary » *Third Saturday after Pentecost*

Dear Jesus, we unite ourselves to you and your Father through the heart of Mary. On this special day, we see Mary's inner joys and sorrows, her love for you and your Father, and her love for all people. It is through the beautiful heart of Mary that we are better able to unite with you, with God our Father, with the Holy Spirit, and with all of humanity. Amen.

Birth of Saint John the Baptist » *June 24*

Creator God, today we celebrate the birth of Saint John the Baptist, who would announce the coming of your Son, Jesus, and baptize him in the Jordan River. John prepared the way for the world to receive your Son. We pray today that we will also be a voice like Saint John the Baptist. Through our words and deeds, we will bring people closer to you. May we be a light for others, bringing you to them, and them to you, so that they may discover the fullness of your love and experience the salvation you offer. Amen.

Saints Peter and Paul » *June 29*

Dear Jesus, today we remember the great works and martyrdom in Rome of Saints Peter and Paul. Peter, your apostle and close friend, whom you made the Rock of your Church, spread your word throughout the empire. And Paul, whom you appeared to and converted after your resurrection, took your message and spread the Good News throughout the Greek world. We thank you, Lord, for the gift of these two great men who made your life and message known throughout the world. Amen.

Saint Thomas » *July 3*

Loving Jesus, like Saint Thomas, we often have doubt. We doubt your reality in our lives, our faith, and our own abilities. These doubts are often a result of fear and insecurity. We pray that these doubts result in a deep search for the truth, ridding us of fear and insecurity and propelling us to discover truth and justice. We pray that we find a deeper prayer life and spiritual journey. Amen.

Our Lady of Peace » *July 9*

Dear God, Mary accepted your will with a peaceful heart, did not respond to your call in anger, and did not retaliate with violence at the crucifixion of her Son. We look to Mary as a model of peace. We live in a world that is always in conflict, often resulting in war and the death of innocence. We pray to be more like Mary. May we accept your will, find compromise in the most difficult of situations, and resolve conflict with peace. Amen.

Saint James » *July 25*

Ever-present Jesus, you chose your apostle Saint James to be with you during the transfiguration and some of your miracles. You chose James, as you have chosen all of us, to share in your mystery and glory. Each and every day, with all the beauty of creation and the majesty of each person, we witness the wonderful things you have done. Jesus, help us so that we do not get entangled in things of no importance. Help us to keep our minds open and free of worry and fear so that we can, like James, witness the beauty of all that you have given us. Amen.

Saints Anne and Joachim » *July 26*

God of love, we look to Saints Anne and Joachim as the model of good parents. They raised their daughter, Mary, the mother of your Son, Jesus, to be a worthy Mother of God. Today, we ask you to give our parents the patience and wisdom to raise their children to be good, kind, and faith-filled people, and we ask that they receive the support they need from family, friends, and community to be a constant source of encouragement and love to their children. Amen.

The Assumption of Mary » *August 15*

Dear Jesus, you took Mary into heaven, both body and soul. She is with you in all your glory. It is our prayer that while we live the gift of life here on earth, we may live with you in your Spirit. We pray that through our own journey, we will able to discover your divine nature within us and will be able to be one with your infinite love, beauty, and wisdom. Amen.

Saint Augustine » *August 28*

Dear God, we give thanks for the gift of Saint Augustine, one of the greatest theological minds of the first thousand years of the church. Saint Augustine helped shape the early church, and he helped us understand your message. He helped us see that your church was a spiritual city of God, different from our earthly city. He helped us understand the concept of the Trinity and many other complicated doctrines. We pray that we will always value our education and dedicate ourselves to our studies so that we too, like Saint Augustine, can be a source of enlightenment to others. Amen.

INTERACTIVE PRAYERS FOR DAILY LIFE

Acceptance

"My Father, if it is possible, let this cup pass from me; yet not what I want but what you want." **MATTHEW 26:39**

What you ask for is not always what you hope for

"I asked for strength that I might achieve; I was made weak that I might learn humbly to obey. I asked for health that I might do great things; I was given infirmity that I might do better things. I asked for riches that I might be happy; I was given poverty that I might be wise. I asked for power that I might have the praise of others; I was given weakness that I might feel the need of God. I asked for all things that I might enjoy life; I was given life that I might enjoy all things. I got nothing that I had asked for but everything that I had hoped for. Almost despite myself my unspoken prayers were answered; I am, among all men and women, most richly blessed." **UNKNOWN CONFEDERATE SOLDIER**

- *Are there times when people ask for things and later regret receiving them?*

- *Does God have a plan for each of us?*

- *Give an example of when accepting is better than trying to fight.*

Let Go and let God

God of peace and acceptance, things do not often go the way we want them to go. We can be disappointed, particularly when we want something really badly and it doesn't work out. We pray today to be granted the ability to accept things that we are not able to change. We pray for peace of mind and heart. Please grant us the faith to trust in you. Help us to follow the words in the Serenity Prayer: "God, grant me the serenity to accept the things I cannot change, courage to change the things I can, and wisdom to know the difference." Amen.

- *Why is it difficult to accept what life gives us?*

- *Is it easy to "let go and let God"? What are the challenges?*

- *When is it best to surrender? When is it best to change the way things are?*

Appreciation

As punished, and yet not killed; as sorrowful, yet always rejoicing; as poor, yet making many rich; as having nothing, and yet possessing everything.
2 CORINTHIANS 6:9–10

Thank God for great people

God of peace and joy, we give you thanks for those people in our lives who have touched us in a special way. We thank them for their acts of kindness, their generosity, their care, and their concern. May they be granted the courage to continue their good works and be blessed with peace and joy. Help us, Lord, to always appreciate those people in our lives who have been there for us. May they know the gratitude that we hold in our hearts. Amen.

- *What are some ways that we can show appreciation for people we care about?*

- *Do we take the little things in life for granted, or do we recognize them as gifts?*

- *Are there people in our lives whom we take for granted?*

Thank you for this day

Dear Creator, we give you thanks for another blessed day. Thank you for the air we breathe, the wondrous nature that surrounds us, and the beautiful people we have in our lives. May we seize this day and live each moment with gratitude and joy. Amen.

- *In what ways can we express our gratitude for each day?*

- *What does it mean to "live life to the fullest"?*

- *Is it difficult to maintain an attitude of gratitude and appreciation?*

Assertiveness

Whoever welcomes this child in my name welcomes me, and whoever welcomes me welcomes the one who sent me; for the least among all of you is the greatest. LUKE 9:48

My opinion counts

Dear Lord, there are times when we are not able to say what we feel. We find it hard to speak up and to be assertive, even when we strongly oppose things. We pray today for the confidence to believe in ourselves and know that our opinion is important and worthy. Grant us the confidence and the strength to believe in ourselves, our opinions, and our ability to make a difference through contributing our input. Amen.

- *Is every person's opinion important? Are some opinions more important than others?*

- *Why do we sometimes think our opinions are not good enough?*

- *Does God value all opinions equally?*

It's time to turn the tables

Dear Jesus, you were the perfect example, demonstrating when to be assertive. You would not compromise your integrity or your convictions. You showed this when you overturned the tables in the Temple and when you stood up to the self-righteous and proud. You taught us to be assertive even when the rights and integrity of our self or others were threatened. Be with us, Jesus, when we need to be assertive, taking a stand for what we believe in and for what is just and right. Amen.

- *Jesus overturned the tables in the Temple. How do we know when to be assertive?*

- *What prevents us from being assertive? How do we overcome these obstacles?*

- *How do we feel about ourselves when we stand up for what we believe in?*

Beauty

The Lord has done great things for us, and we rejoiced. **PSALM 126:3**

Nice Weather; God is good

God of blessings, we take a moment today to say thank you for your love and your blessings. Nature causes us to pause and to take notice of your wonderful majesty. May we never lose sight of the love you have for us and the beauty of your creation. Let our hearts be filled with joy. Amen.

- *What are things in nature that bring you closer to God?*

- *Do we often miss signs of God's majesty in our world? Why?*

- *What can help us to take the time to appreciate all the wonder of our world?*

All is beautiful

God of wonder and beauty, help us to see the beauty that surrounds us—the sky, the sun, the rain, the air we breathe, the ground we walk on, the trees and plants, the animals, and the colors of your creation. May we take the time to appreciate every detail of your creation. Amen.

- *What prevents us from seeing the simple but beautiful things around us?*

- *How can we learn to slow down and appreciate these gifts?*

- *How will appreciating God's creation benefit our everyday life and our outlook on life?*

Body, Mind, and Soul

May the God of peace himself sanctify you entirely; and may your spirit and soul and body be kept sound and blameless at the coming of our Lord Jesus Christ. **1 THESSALONIANS 5:23**

Care for self and others

Dear Jesus, we know that it is not right to mistreat others or to be mistreated, whether it be verbally, emotionally, or physically. This is destructive to the mind, body, and spirit. We pray that we become a healing people, just as you healed those you walked with on earth. May we learn to be kind and gentle, tender and loving. Like you, Jesus, we will bring out the very best in others and in ourselves when we are a healing people. Amen.

- *What can we do to recognize when we are being treated poorly or treating others poorly?*

- *What events in Jesus' life demonstrate how to treat others and how we should be treated?*

- *What are some specific things we can do to show kindness in a relationship?*

A prayer for healing

Dear Lord, we see how destructive addictions and other unhealthy behaviors can be. We pray today for all those who do not see themselves as worthy or capable of living a healthy, productive life. We pray that they will see how much you love them and how much they are loved by others. We pray that they will recognize how worthy they are to be successful, healthy, and happy. We pray that they will shake off all self-doubt and poor self-image so that they can excel and be the persons you call them to be. Amen.

- *Why do some people treat themselves so poorly?*

- *What makes it hard to recognize how much God loves us?*

- *What can we do to affirm the beauty and goodness in others?*

Bullying

Only, live your life in a manner worthy of the gospel of Christ, so that, whether I come and see you or am absent and hear about you, I will know that you are standing firm in one spirit, striving side by side with one mind for the faith of the gospel, and are in no way intimidated by your opponents.
PHILIPPIANS 1:27–28

Who do they think they are?
Kind God, we do not understand why some people think they are better than others and get some kind of "thrill" by making others feel weak. We do not understand how people can get away with treating others like they are less worthy. We pray for the victims, that they may always know that they are worthy of respect. We pray for the offenders, that they may be granted healing from their malicious ways. We pray for the bystanders, that they may have the courage to step up and take a stand against disrespectful and hateful behavior. Help us, dear God, to live in peace, respecting and caring for one another, as your Son has taught us. Amen.

- *Why do some people bully others?*

- *How can we help the bullies to see that what they are doing is wrong?*

- *What can we do in our communities to prevent bullying?*

Cyber-bullying

Dear Lord, we are very fortunate to have technological advancements, and we give thanks for this technology. However, we also pray for those who use social media and other technology to gossip, slander, criticize others, and send hateful messages. May they be healed of their malice and hate. We pray that they realize their sinful acts and be converted to ways of peace and harmony. We pray that the victims of cyber-bullying realize that what is being said about them is not true and is solely a reflection of the anger and hate in the sender. Amen.

- *Do you think that bullies should be charged by the police?*

- *Do people who are being bullied feel comfortable asking for help?*

- *What can school staff do to correct any bullying that is taking place in the school?*

Caring

We who are strong ought to put up with the failings of the weak, and not to please ourselves. Each of us must please our neighbor for the good purpose of building up the neighbor. ROMANS 15:1–2

Helping one another

Dear Jesus, we pray today for the faith to follow your example of caring and serving others. Be with us when we reach out to our friends who are in need so that we can provide the support and care they need to make their difficult times easier. Be with us when we make the efforts to empower them to believe in themselves and the gifts you have given them. Amen.

- *Do we see a person who is caring for others as a weak person or a strong person?*

- *Does society encourage us to put ourselves first or the needs of others first?*

- *Does the desire to help one another come naturally or do we have to work on it?*

I need some TLC

Dear Jesus, we are at a place now where we feel the need for support from our friends. We do not want to talk about our problems; we simply want people to be there for us. Help us, Jesus, during this time, to know that our friends care about us and that you walk beside us. Help us to see that we are not alone, and grant us the courage to lean on others. Amen.

- *Do we all have times in our lives when all we see is darkness? Where can we find help?*

- *Would prayer help us to see that there is light in the midst of this darkness?*

- *Is it difficult to ask friends, family, or teachers for help? Why?*

Chastity

Shun youthful passions and pursue righteousness, faith, love, and peace, along with those who call on the Lord from a pure heart. **2 TIMOTHY 2:22**

My body is a temple

Dear God, you have made us in your image. You have given to us a mind, body, and soul with great potential to do good. May all that we think and do reflect the beauty of your creation and the building of your kingdom. We strive to treat our bodies as a sacred temple, maintaining good health. We work at developing our minds through the acquisition of knowledge to know truth and justice. And our souls desire to be one with you, acquiring a purity of heart. Amen.

- *Do we treat our bodies with respect? If so, how? If not, why?*

- *Does society promote us treating our bodies with respect?*

- *What are some things we can do to nurture our mind and spirit?*

Lord, help me to stay strong

Dear Lord, in satisfying personal desires, we often neglect our mental and spiritual health. Lord, we pray for the gift of temperance so that we will have the strength to refrain from all that will harm us. You have taught us that we have infinite potential, each of us gifted, and we pray that all we do reflects and gives glory for the gifts you gave us. We stand back and look at ourselves in awe of the beauty you have created. With your grace, we can make our lives beautiful and wonderful gifts to our community and the world. Amen.

- *Why do some people have difficulty seeing the beautiful gift that they are?*

- *What does it mean to have the gift of temperance?*

- *What are some of the ingredients needed to forge strong relationships?*

Church

For just as the body is one and has many members, and all the members of the body, though many, are one body, so it is with Christ. For in the one Spirit we were all baptized into one body...and we were all made to drink of one Spirit. **1 CORINTHIANS 12:12–13**

We are the church

Dear Lord, we pray that we may come to understand that we are the church. We are filled with gifts and talents of which the church is in need. Help us to understand that the church is not separate and apart from us. We are church, and the more we become involved and share our gifts, the more effective and meaningful the church will be. Help us, Lord, to use our gifts to be an awesome church. Amen.

- *What does it mean to say "We are the church"?*

- *Do young people feel they are an important part of the church?*

- *What can the school and the parish do to help us get more involved in church?*

The church needs us

Dear Lord, often we do not realize how much we are needed. You have blessed us with amazing gifts and strengths. Help us to recognize that we have a great deal to contribute to the church. Help us to know that our gifts will make a big difference in making the church come alive for so many youth. We pray today that all youth will recognize how much the church would benefit from their full and active participation. May we be forever willing to take up this challenge and get involved. Amen.

- *Do young people feel that their church welcomes them? Why or why not?*

- *What can the church do to help youth become more involved?*

- *What can youth offer the church? Are their contributions valued and needed?*

Class Presentations

Be strong in the Lord and in the strength of his power. Put on the whole armor of God. **EPHESIANS 6:10–11A**

Calm, cool, and collected

Dear Lord, as the class begins with presentations, we pray that you bless us all. Help us to overcome fear and be confident in what we are about to present. May we each be respectful of one another during the presentations, giving our full attention and support to those who are giving presentations. Amen.

- *What are some strategies to stay calm during presentations?*

■ *Why is it that we sometimes doubt ourselves?*

■ *Getting up and talking in front of others is a common fear.*
  Why is that?

We hate presentations

Dear Lord, we do not like getting up in front of the class and presenting. We feel nervous and scared. Help us to overcome these feelings as we make our presentations. We do not know where these feelings come from. We only know that they are there and that we do not like these feelings. Lord, grant us a sense of calm so that we may make a presentation that truly reflects what we know and what we hope to convey.
Amen.

■ *What makes classroom presentations so difficult?*

■ *If someone has a hard time with presentations, is it fair*
  to make them do them?

■ *Is fear a helpful emotion? Why?*

Class Trip

Above all, maintain constant love for one another,
for love covers a multitude of sins. Be hospitable to one another
without complaining. **1 PETER 4:8–9**

The time of our lives

Dear God, we give you thanks for the opportunity to take this trip. As we are about to begin on our journey, we pray for a safe ride. We ask you to bless our driver and our supervisors. May we be appreciative of their efforts in providing us with this opportunity, and we ask for the strength and discipline to demonstrate our appreciation in and through our good behavior. Amen.

- *What makes a trip awesome?*

- *What can ruin a trip?*

- *What can we do to ensure everyone loves the trip and benefits from it?*

We give thanks for this day

Dear Lord, each and every day is a blessing. Today, we have an opportunity to learn about ourselves, others, and the place we visit. We ask you to watch over us on our trip today. Keep our eyes open to see the beauty of your creation, our ears keen to hear the sounds of life, and our hearts full of love to receive all that you will offer. Amen.

- *Do we view today's trip as a blessing? Why? Why not?*

- *What attitude do we need to adopt to bring the greatest meaning to this trip?*

- *Do we see today as an opportunity to get to know someone we do not yet know?*

Clubs/Teams (Joining)

[You are] fearfully and wonderfully made. **PSALM 139:14**

Let's get in the game

God of strength, many of us would really like to be in clubs and on teams but are afraid to try out. We may feel that people are selected before tryouts begin. Sometimes we fear that people will speak critically about us when we try out. Some of us feel people will talk about us if we don't make the team. Lord, help us to see that no matter the outcome, it is in trying that we succeed. Help us to overcome all fears and to be proud of ourselves for having the courage to try. Amen.

- *Are teams and club members chosen fairly? If not, why?*

- *What can be done to encourage students to try out for teams and clubs?*

- *Are there very talented people in school who won't try out for a team? Why?*

I didn't make it

God of hope, it is not easy getting cut. You feel like everyone is talking about you behind your back. Help us to get through this period with confidence and hope. May this experience not cause anyone to stop trying. Help us to realize that it takes more courage to try and to get cut, than to not show up at all. May we be proud of our willingness to put ourselves forward, and may we continue to be confident in our talents and abilities. Amen.

- *One tries and gets cut; another does not try for fear of getting cut. Which do you admire more?*

- *What can we do to help support people who get cut?*

- *Who are some successful people who failed many times before their success?*

Commitment

Whatever you do, work at it with all your heart, as though you were working for the Lord and not for people. **COLOSSIANS 3:23 (GOOD NEWS TRANSLATION)**

Commitment is key

Dear God, help us to be committed to all those aspects of our lives that are in need of our attention and gifts. When we agree to be a part of some group, project, team, or club, grant us the discipline and the wisdom we need to make our commitment real and meaningful. Keep us focused and on track so that we can reach our goals and feel good about the contributions we have made. Amen.

- *Is it important to keep commitments in every situation? Why or why not?*

- *When we do not keep our commitments, does it affect our reputation or character?*

- *What commitment did Jesus make and stick to, even when it brought great suffering?*

Keep us committed

Dear Jesus, we are inspired by your commitment to your mission, to your followers, and to your Father in heaven. Your commitment brought you great suffering. It also made your life rich, full of meaning, joy, and hope. Your commitment changed the world. We pray that we can emulate this kind of commitment to our own family, friends, and mission. Grant us the courage, strength, determination, and fortitude to be faithful to our own commitments. Amen.

- *When are we required to make a commitment?*

- *How do we stay committed when it gets tough?*

- *If we fail at keeping a commitment, can we go back and try again? Why? Why not?*

Community

"Every kingdom divided against itself is laid waste, and no city or house divided against itself will stand." **MATTHEW 12:25**

It's up to you!

The following prayer was written by St. Teresa of Ávila. Her words encourage us to go out and do good things in our school, in our community, and in the world. She tells us that it is up to us to bring the love, compassion, kindness, and awareness of Jesus to others: "Christ has no body now but yours; no hands, no feet on earth but yours. Yours are the eyes through which he looks with compassion on this world. Yours are the feet with which he walks to do good. Yours are the hands with which he blesses all the world. Christ has no body now on earth but yours." Amen.

- *Is our school community caring and supportive?*

- *Are there people who feel unwelcomed and unloved?*

- *What can we do in our community so each person feels that he or she belongs?*

We are each other's keeper

Dear God, you sent us your only Son because of the unconditional and abundant love you have for each and every one of us. Help us here at (*name of school*) to be instruments of your love and your peace. May all that we do create an atmosphere where every person in this building feels your love, support, guidance, and care through each of our actions. Give us the courage and strength to reach out and respond to your invitation to be peacemakers and people of love. Amen.

- *How are we responding to the challenge to build God's kingdom in this community?*

- *How do we recognize those in our community who are alone, rejected, or depressed?*

- *What can we do to follow the example of Jesus in creating a caring community?*

Compassion

"In everything do to others as you would have them do to you; for this is the law and the prophets." **MATTHEW 7:12**

Let's feel the love

Loving Jesus, we are often in awe when we look at the compassion and mercy that you demonstrated during your life on earth. You reached out to the downtrodden, the sinner, the loner, the leper, and the rejected. You did not judge these people; instead you showed your love and the love of your Father. Grant us the ability to reach out to all who are in need. May we refrain from judging, gossip, and criticizing others. Amen.

- *Jesus accepted people whom society did not. How can we follow his example?*

- *Can you list five virtues that Jesus lived out while on earth?*

- *Is it possible to follow Jesus and live a life where we never judge others?*

Putting others first

Dear Lord, it is sometimes difficult to be compassionate, rising above ourselves to love and serve others, especially when we are too caught up in our own lives. We pray that no matter what difficulties we face or what obstacles we have to overcome, we will always be able to rise above ourselves to love and serve others and to be open to the love they give to us. We know that it is this compassion for others, like your compassion for us, that will make our lives rich with peace. Amen.

- *What does it mean to "put others first"?*

- *Is it harder to put others first when we are dealing with problems in our own lives?*

- *What are the joys we experience when we put others first?*

Computers

Prudence will watch over you; and understanding will guard you. **PROVERBS 2:11**

We love our computers

Dear Lord, we give you thanks for so many things that offer us fun and excitement. We love our time on our computers. It enables us to communicate with friends, follow celebrities, keep up with current events, and watch movies and videos. We pray that we always use computers in a way that makes us and others better people. Help us to use our computers to empower ourselves and others through acquiring knowledge, exercising our talents, and building a better world. Amen.

- *Should adults be concerned with how much time we spend on computers?*

- *Are we tempted to do things on the computer that we know are not the best for us?*

- *What can we do to ensure that our time on computers is what's best for us and others?*

Things done on computers can be hurtful

Dear Lord, we know the benefits of computers. We are able to formulate assignments, obtain research, and send information. However, sometimes computers are used in ways that can be harmful to ourselves and hurtful to others. Harmful videos can be posted, rumors can be created, and lies can be spread, all in a matter of moments. It is all easy and tempting, even though the damage we do is often irreparable. Lord, we pray for discretion and that your word guide all that we do on the computer. Amen.

- *Why do people post things that can hurt others?*

- *What can be done to prevent people from posting destructive comments and material?*

- *In what ways can the computer be used to serve others and build a better world?*

Confidence

See what love the Father has given us that we should be called children of God; and that is what we are. **1 JOHN 3:1**

You are a child of God

Prayer attributed to Saint Thérèse of Lisieux
and to Saint Teresa of Ávila
"May today there be peace within. May you trust God that you are exactly where you are meant to be. May you not forget the infinite possibilities that are born of faith. May you use those gifts that you have received and pass on the love that has been given to you. May you be content knowing you are a child of God. Let this presence settle into your bones, and allow your soul the freedom to sing, dance, praise, and love. It is there for each and every one of us." Amen.

- *How does having confidence help us achieve our potential?*

- *Are there brilliant and talented people who go unnoticed because they lack confidence?*

- *What does it take to give confidence to someone?*

Let us show them what we've got

Dear Lord, in a world that is often suspicious of young people, we find it difficult to be confident in our abilities and gifts. We pray today that we may be blessed with the confidence that enables us to express our gifts and talents. May we know that our gifts come from you and that you would like nothing more than for us to develop and use our gifts to the best of our abilities. We pray for confidence, so that we can contribute the great gifts that we have. Amen.

- *How do we attain and maintain confidence?*

- *What is the difference between confidence and conceit?*

- *How can we help others develop their gifts?*

Cooperation

But take thought for what is noble in the sight of all. If it is possible, so far as it depends on you, live peaceably with all. **ROMANS 12:17B–18**

Let's work together

Dear Lord, we know that each of us is different. We have different gifts, different tastes, different likes, and different dreams. Help us this school year to work together. We know that when we cooperate with one another, we will achieve far more than we would working in isolation. Grant us the gifts we require to be a strong group, able to work together, complementing each other, and accomplishing great things. Amen.

- *What are the necessary ingredients to successfully work together?*

- *What are the challenges of working together?*

- *In what ways are we better when we work together as a team?*

Let's rise above ourselves

Dear Lord, it is difficult to cooperate with others when they think differently and act selfishly. We pray that we will have the wisdom to put aside our personal views and opinions, our biases and prejudices, so that we can rise above our own egos. We know that when we work in a spirit of cooperation, great things will happen.

Help us to make great things happen together. Amen.

- *What are the advantages of working with someone else?*

- *How can we ensure that each person is able to contribute their gifts in a group?*

- *What are some of the virtues we see in an effective group?*

Courage

Keep alert, stand firm in the faith, be courageous, be strong.
Let all that you do be done in love. **1 CORINTHIANS 16:13–14**

Let's take a stand!

God of courage and wisdom, today we pray that we too might have courage and wisdom. These gifts serve us well and help us in serving others. Things happen very quickly, and we must make decisions within seconds. May we always choose the path that will make us most proud. We also pray for the gift of courage. It is not always easy to be the first to speak up, to step in, or to put an end to things that we believe are unjust. We pray to make choices that reflect our true character, ones that focus on serving you and, in so doing, helping each other. Amen.

- *Do most youth have the courage to stand up to their peers when they pressure them?*

- *Are we born with courage and wisdom or do we acquire them with age?*

- *What are ways we can acquire the gifts of wisdom and courage?*

Go get 'em, tiger

Dear Lord, we are often called to take risks and to put ourselves on the line. We pray today for the wonderful gift of courage. This gift will enable us to go after things that we may not feel capable of attaining. This gift will enable us to take a stand against things we do not believe in. May we be filled with courage as we attempt to live out the gospel values. We ask this through you, Lord, our hero and our friend. Amen.

- *Jesus demonstrated great courage. How can we model his courage?*

- *Are there times in life when we feel more courageous than others? When?*

- *Are there times when we need to demonstrate our courage more than others? When?*

Creativity

"In the same way, let your light shine before others, so that they may see your good works and give glory to your Father in heaven." MATTHEW 5:16

We are creative

Dear Lord, thank you for the gift of creativity. Help us to believe in our own ideas and inspirations, whether they be in writing, art, music, drama, dance, or (*add your own creative gift here*). Sometimes we are afraid to express ourselves for fear of others. Help us ignore those who scoff at our creative gifts. Help us to get over those things that prevent us from being expressive and creative. May we be granted confidence so that we can develop and express the wondrous gifts with which we have been blessed. Amen.

- *Does jealousy from another person prevent people from being creative?*

- *Who are some people in history who were so creative they changed the world?*

- *Is there sufficient support in our community, and in our families, for us to be creative?*

Time to contribute

Dear Lord, what a great gift you gave to us when you gave us creativity. This gift, given to all of us in different ways, allows us to contribute to the world and make it a better place. We pray that the creativity you gave us will always be used for the good of humanity, bringing peace and prosperity to all. When others do not recognize what we have to offer, we know that you will be with us as we strive to create a better world. Amen.

- *What are examples of using our creativity for the "good of humanity"?*

- *What are areas in need of creativity within our society and our own school community?*

- *Everyone is creative in some way. In what areas are you creative?*

Criticism

Those who passed by derided him, shaking their heads and saying, "You who would destroy the temple and built it in three days, save yourself! If you are the Son of God, come down from that cross." **MATTHEW 27:39-40**

Let's rise above the criticism

Dear God, help us to never be discouraged by the criticism of others. When people say terrible and hurtful things about us, help us to remain focused on our mission, the same way that Jesus remained focused on his mission. Grant us strength in times of ridicule, confidence in times of doubt, and faith in times of trial. Amen.

- *Why do people criticize others?*

- *How can we best deal with criticism?*

- *How can we continue to move forward when we are being criticized?*

We shall not get discouraged

Dear Lord, when criticism is constructive and done in a good spirit, we pray to be open to it, allowing it to transform us into better people. At the same time, Lord, some people will criticize us because they are jealous, threatened, or ignorant. Give us the clarity of mind and the strength to rise above the criticisms of others so that we may continue on our path to doing good works and accomplishing great things. Amen.

- *How do we know if criticism is constructive (helpful) or destructive?*

- *Does getting the opinion of others help us to be more or less creative?*

- *How does constructive criticism help us grow and develop?*

Dances/Prom

He called a child, whom he put among them, and said, "Truly I tell you, unless you change and become like children, you will never enter the kingdom of heaven." **MATTHEW 18:2-3**

Let's dance the night away

God of blessings, we are excited about the dance/prom and look forward to having a great deal of fun. We are grateful for the gifts of music and dance. Thank you for the opportunities we have in life to celebrate and relax. We pray in gratitude for the gift of our friends and our community. May we never lose our youthful joy, viewing all of life as a celebration and an opportunity to be happy. Amen.

- *Are young people forced to grow up too fast?*

- *Do youth need more opportunities to be themselves and simply have fun?*

- *What is it about dances/proms that is most liked?*

Let it be a great night

Dear Lord, dances/proms are not always easy. We know a great deal of effort is put into making this dance/prom possible. We are thankful for those who did the work to make this possible and to all those who will be working this evening and cleaning up afterwards. We also pray that all those attending will experience an evening filled with joy, offering opportunities to renew friendships and meet new people. Amen.

- *What are some things that may make an evening like this difficult for some students?*

- *Why do some students not want to attend an evening like this?*

- *What kinds of pressure do youth face when attending a prom or dance?*

Dating

For everything there is a season, and a time for every matter under heaven.
ECCLESIASTES 3:1

Becoming a better person

Dear Lord, may our dating be an opportunity to elevate ourselves and others to be better people. We pray that through dating we will come to appreciate ourselves and others as your children. Help us to conduct ourselves in ways that are respectful and appreciative of the life you have given us. We hope that whomever we meet and enter into relationship with will accept us and respect us for who we are. In turn, may we appreciate them for who they are. Amen.

- *Is there pressure in relationships to be someone other than who we are?*

- *Should someone compromise who they are to satisfy the person they are dating?*

- *In what ways can dating help us become better people?*

Finding the right person

Dear Lord, we pray that we will find people who will bring out the best in us, people who help us to shine as you have created us to shine. May we be blessed with the mind and heart to direct us to people who make us more loving, compassionate, and forgiving. May we be attracted to people who help us be the people you created us to be. Amen.

- *What are some of the qualities people should have to build strong relationships?*

- *How does being in a healthy relationship make persons feel about themselves?*

- *Why is the virtue of patience so important in finding a healthy relationship?*

Death

I want to know Christ and the power of his resurrection and the sharing of his sufferings by becoming like him in his death, if somehow I may attain the resurrection from the dead. **PHILIPPIANS 3:10–11**

Why do young people die?

Lord, we are devastated by the death of *(name of person)*. We find it difficult to deal with tragedies of this magnitude. It feels as if this is not real and we do not know what to say or do. Lord, we pray for *(name of person)*. May she/he be at complete peace and joy with you in heaven. We pray for the family. Although there is no making sense of this death, we pray that the Holy Spirit will be with them, empowering them with all that they need to get through this most difficult time. May they also find comfort through the gestures of love offered to them from a loving community. Amen.

- *What are things we can do to help ourselves and friends when they are grieving?*

- *Are those who have died still with us? If so, in what way?*

- *Is there comfort in the knowledge that Jesus offers us the resurrection?*

They live on in our hearts

Dear God, we thank you for the wonderful memories we have of our departed loved ones. We are grateful when these memories bring us happiness and comfort. Help us to continue to keep the memories of our loved ones alive by living out the gifts and virtues we treasured so much in their lives. May our remembering of them in this way help their spirit to live on in us, and may their virtues contribute to building your kingdom here on earth. Amen.

- *Does Jesus' death and resurrection, and the promise of eternal life, help with grief?*

- *Does the school community offer enough support throughout the grieving process?*

- *How do the memories of a lost loved one help us through difficult times?*

Decision Making

"Truly I tell you, whatever you bind on earth will be bound in heaven, and whatever you loose on earth will be loosed in heaven." **MATTHEW 18:18**

It's a tough decision

Lord, the teenage years are not always easy. We are faced with many different dilemmas. There are important decisions to make. It is not always clear what decision we should make. We pray today for the guidance of the Holy Spirit so that the decisions we make are the very best for our spiritual, mental, and physical well-being. May we remain open to the Spirit and have the courage and discipline to make good decisions. Amen.

- *What questions do we need to ask ourselves when we are making important decisions?*

- *Should we consult others to help us make decisions? If so, who?*

- *How do we know when we have made a good decision?*

Lord, grant me wisdom

God of wisdom, decision making can be difficult and complex. We must consider many factors, because the result will impact us as well as others. We sometimes feel lost, confused, and stressed. Grant us wisdom and a sense of calm that enables us to think logically and clearly. We look to you in making our decisions, Lord. Amen.

- *How do we overcome stress and confusion when we are making a decision?*

- *How do we know that we have the necessary knowledge and considered all the options?*

- *Do we make decisions based on what we believe to be right or what others want?*

Determination

Do not lag in zeal, be ardent in spirit, serve the Lord. **ROMANS 12:11**

No one is stopping us

Dear God, bless us with the strength, discipline, and courage to develop our gifts. Keep us confident in the face of adversity, determined in the face of defeat, and optimistic in the face of pressure. As we work to be the best that we can be, keep us faith-filled and joy-filled. May we always, first and foremost, use our gifts to serve you and to build one human family here on earth. Amen.

- *Is it easy to develop our gifts? Does the community provide support?*

- *How do we stay determined when others put us down or reject our gifts?*

- *Why do we tend to put emphasis on the negative comments and not the positive?*

Never give up

Dear Lord, we are often faced with obstacles that seem too great to overcome. We pray today for the gifts of dedication and perseverance. No matter what is ahead of us, whether it be exams, presentations, friendship issues, athletic challenges, or our part-time jobs, help us soldier on and never give up. Help us to attain our goals, even when they seem impossible. Help us to never give in to defeat. Amen.

- *What do people do when they feel like giving up? What motivates them to keep trying?*

- *How did Jesus feel when he was rejected, even by his closest followers?*

- *What enabled Jesus to continue to carry his cross and endure his crucifixion?*

Diligence

Commit your life to the Lord; trust in him, and he will act. **PSALM 37:5**

The early bird gets the worm

Dear Lord, diligence is a wonderful gift. It enables us to go after things we want to accomplish. Through diligence, we are able to do our best, whether it be studying for an exam, attempting to secure a part-time job, or working to attain a personal best. No matter what we are after, Lord, we pray for the gift of diligence. We know that through hard work, persistence, and your presence, we will be better able to attain our dreams. Amen.

- *Do some people have a better work ethic than others? Why or why not?*

- *What is it that enables us to remain diligent and steadfast in what we are doing?*

- *Is it important to never give up? Are there times when we need to "throw in the towel"?*

Help us get it done

Lord, we are often overwhelmed with everything that we need to do and all that is expected of us. We have our school work, part-time jobs, chores at home, and commitments to teams and clubs. Help us to be patient with ourselves, to never get overwhelmed or anxious. With calmness, discipline, and the diligence we pray for, with you at our side, we are sure to complete all our tasks with success. Amen.

- *Is too much expected of us? If so, what can we do about it?*

- *How do we prioritize and find the proper balance?*

- *What are some of the obstacles that get in our way and prevent us from being diligent?*

Discernment

"No one can serve two masters; for a slave will either hate the one and love the other or be devoted to one and despise the other. You cannot serve God and wealth." **MATTHEW 6:24**

Finding our way

As we face our day-to-day lives, we are confronted with many decisions. Today we reflect on Saint Paul's words in his letter to the Philippians (4:8–9; New Living Translation): "And now, dear brothers and sisters, one final thing. Fix your thoughts on what is true, and honorable, and right and pure, and lovely, and admirable. Think about things that are excellent and worthy of praise. Keep putting into practice all you learned and received from me—everything you heard from me and saw me doing. Then the God of peace will always be with you." Amen.

- *What does Saint Paul mean?*

- *How are we able to come to know what is "true, honorable and right"?*

- *How do we know when we are on the right path?*

Help me find the way

Dear Lord, we often find it difficult to know what to choose and how to respond to many situations in our lives. Give us the discipline to acquire the knowledge we need to make good decisions. Grant us the ability and willingness to open our minds and hearts to the Holy Spirit as well as to follow the path upon which we are led. We also pray that we use the gift of prudence to discern between that which is constructive and that which is destructive. Amen.

- *Is the Holy Spirit always present?*

- *How can we hear the voice of the Holy Spirit? What do we need to do?*

- *Where do we find the strength to follow the guidance of the Holy Spirit?*

Driver's License

And remember, I am always with you, to the end of the age.

MATTHEW 28:20B

Get me on the road

Dear Lord, as we prepare to apply for a driver's license, we pray that our test will go well. Help us to be calm from the moment we get into the car. May we not experience any difficult obstacles on the route and be clear minded so that we remember all the rules of the road. Lord, we pray that we pass this test. Amen.

- *What strategies can we use to stay calm on our driving test?*

- *What are some tips to help us remain calm in any stressful situation?*

- *Is our anxiety because we are afraid of driving or afraid of failing?*

I need to relax

Dear God, driving is very exciting, and it is a great joy to drive with friends. We pray that we will always be responsible drivers, respectful of the car we are in, respectful of the passengers we carry, respectful of other drivers and pedestrians. We ask you, God, to watch over all of us, keeping us safe. Amen.

- *Why do we get so stressed when we take our driving test?*

- *What is the best way to stay focused?*

- *Do you think prayer helps? If so, how?*

Education

I pray that you may have the power to comprehend, with all the saints, what is the breadth and length and height and depth, and to know the love of Christ that surpasses knowledge, so that you may be filled with all the fullness of God. EPHESIANS 3:18–19

Putting our education to good use

Dear God, we give you thanks for the opportunity to learn. Although we may sometimes complain about going to school, we know that we are blessed to receive an education. Keep alive within us all that we have learned. Help us to be willing to use our knowledge to create a better world and a more perfect and just society. Amen.

- *Do students in general see education as a great gift and opportunity to better their lives?*

- *In what ways can education give us the tools to change the world?*

- *How do we have a responsibility to use our knowledge to serve others?*

We are stressed

Dear Lord, when we get overwhelmed with our workload, get tired of studying and completing assignments, and prefer to have the semester end, give us a renewed enthusiasm. Help us to dedicate ourselves to our studies so that we can perform to the best of our ability. We pray to know, no matter how overwhelmed we get, that you are always there with us and that our hard work will pay off. Amen.

- *Knowing how difficult school can be, how can we remain appreciative of our education?*

- *What can we do to appreciate education when we are experiencing work overload?*

- *How do we show appreciation to parents and staff who go beyond the call of duty?*

Elderly

Let the elders who rule well be considered worthy of double honor.

1 TIMOTHY 5:17

Show love to the elderly

Dear Lord, when people ignore and undermine the ability of the elderly, they dismiss the wonderful gifts that they have to offer. Help us, Lord, to appreciate the phenomenal gifts and wisdom of the elderly. Help us to make them know and feel the value we hold for them, the gratitude we hold for the lives they have lived, and the admiration we hold for what they offer us through their wisdom and experience. Amen.

- *Do we treat the elderly with respect?*

- *What gifts do the elderly have to offer that we do not have?*

- *In what ways can we show our love to our elderly?*

Let's comfort the lonely

God, grant us a giving heart so that we may take time to comfort those who are alone and lonely. We pray for the elderly, particularly those who are alone and sad. May we take time to visit them, cheer them up, and show them our gratitude so that they feel loved and cared for. May we never lose sight of their suffering. Propel us to action on their behalf. Amen.

- *When we visit the elderly does our visit bring them comfort?*

- *What are things that we can do to make the elderly feel appreciated?*

- *What are some of the organizations we can volunteer at to assist the elderly?*

Embracing Everyone

"You have heard that it was said, 'You shall love your neighbor and hate your enemy.' But I say to you, Love your enemies and pray for those who persecute you." MATTHEW 5:43–44

Let's live the love of Jesus

Kind God, today we reflect on the gift of your Son. When we look at his example, we know that each of us is called to a life of service and compassion. He did not associate with the rich and established. Rather, he chose to spend time with the lowly and the outcast. Help us to live in solidarity with the people that Jesus chose to spend time with. May our actions help create a world where love prevails. We pray that we have the courage, strength, and wisdom to respond to this call, fully and completely. Amen.

- *Why did Jesus spend so much time with the suffering, sick, and downtrodden?*

- *What was Jesus' main message in the associations he chose?*

- *What are the words that we would use to best describe Jesus?*

Living as one human family

God of all, who is our brother? Who is our sister? You taught us that all people, from all walks of life, from all religions and cultures, are our brothers and sisters. We desire to hold all people in our arms, embracing them and loving them as our brothers and sisters: feeding the hungry, freeing the oppressed, healing the sick, and loving the outcast. Help us, Lord, to live as one human family. Amen.

- *What does it mean to live as brothers and sisters to each other?*

- *What are the things that prevent us from living as brother and sister?*

- *How different would the world be if everyone lived as brother and sister?*

End of Semester

Let the word of Christ dwell in you richly. **COLOSSIANS 3:16A**

Be with us, Lord

Dear God, as we head toward the conclusion of this semester, help us to keep our perspective. Bring us a sense of calm so that we can study to the best of our ability. Provide us with confidence so that we can perform strongly on our tests. Give us discipline so that we can prepare properly and thoroughly. Instill faith in us so that we remain confident in what we have to offer. Be with us as we journey through this challenging and stressful time. Help us to successfully complete our tests and exams and show the world how talented and brilliant we are. Amen.

- *What helps to provide us with a sense of calm?*

- *Does being nervous help us in any way in our performance?*

- *What strategies can we exercise to help us perform to the best of our ability?*

Let's chill with an end-of-semester blessing

Dear God, as we embark upon one of the busiest and most stressful times of the year, we pray that you grant to all of us and our teachers a sense of calm and comfort. As we work hard to complete our culminating assignments and prepare for exams, grant us the discipline to persevere and the confidence to attain our personal best. Amen.

- *When things get tough what can we do to remind us that God is with us?*

- *Building good character is better than building good marks. Do you agree?*

- *Can praying help us to better focus on our schoolwork? If so, how?*

Enthusiasm

Do all things without murmuring and arguing, so that you may be blameless and innocent, children of God. PHILIPPIANS 2:14–15

Remaining enthusiastic despite discouragement

Lord, it is difficult to remain enthusiastic when people do not support us. We find it difficult to remain focused when people create problems and criticize our work. Lord, grant us the wisdom to see the value of what we do. Grant us enthusiasm so that we can complete our work with excellence and pride. Be with us as we walk our journey, determined and enthused to exercise our gifts and share them with the community. Amen.

- *Why do people find it so difficult to always remain enthused?*

- *How does our enthusiasm affect those around us?*

- *What is the best way to handle other people who attempt to diminish our enthusiasm?*

Keeping it positive

Jesus, your enthusiasm spread throughout Galilee, causing thousands to come to hear you preach. We pray that we will always be enthusiastic in all that we do, approaching all with a positive attitude, excited about our work and mission. We call upon the Holy Spirit to always be with us, keeping us enthusiastic about the great gifts we have to offer and about our mission to spread the Good News to build your kingdom on earth. Amen.

- *How do we keep positive and enthusiastic?*

- *What are the benefits to remaining positive and enthused?*

- *Does being enthusiastic make those around us more enthused?*

Environment

So faith by itself, if it has no works, is dead...You see that a person is justified by works and not by faith alone. **JAMES 2:17, 24**

Let's keep the earth clean

Creator God, when we look around at your creation, we are in awe. The flowers, the mountains, the oceans, the gentle breeze— everything we see gives us a glimpse of your majesty. Help us to treat the earth with respect and gratitude. May we be trustworthy keepers of your creation, ensuring that the earth is protected and preserved. Amen.

- *Do we take proper care of our world? Why or why not?*

- *Does this school community respond to the call to take care of God's creation? How?*

- *What can we do to encourage others to be protective of our environment?*

Let's take action

Lord, we care about the beauty of this earth. We treasure the gift of your creation. Give to us the mindfulness to show our gratitude for nature. Let us be more concerned with what we need and less concerned with what we want. Give us the self-discipline not to be wasteful with food, clothing, and all material possessions. Let us be mindful of our waste so that we will find the patience and time to recycle and avoid, in our own small way, polluting this beautiful world you have given us. Amen.

- *What are some examples of people polluting the earth?*

- *Does our desire for material things override our concern for the environment?*

- *What can we do within this school to promote our appreciation for the beauty of nature?*

Exams

I can do all things through [Christ] who strengthens me. **PHILIPPIANS 4:13**

Help us feel your presence, Lord, as we prepare for our exams

Dear God, we thank you for the challenges in our life. Challenges like exams push us to work hard and excel. We thank you for being with us, bringing us a sense of calm when we are confronted with challenges. We have done our work preparing, and now we turn to you because we know you can offer us a calm mind and spirit during this stressful time. Amen.

- *Do we appreciate challenges in our lives, or do we try to avoid them because of stress?*

- *Do we bring this stress on ourselves?*

- *What are some techniques we can use to lessen our stress?*

Help!

Dear God, support and inspire us as we prepare to take this exam. May we feel calm knowing that you are here with us. Help us to recall all that we have studied, doing the best we can to prepare ourselves for this challenge. We pray for self-awareness—to know that when we try our very best, we have already succeeded. When we accept and face challenges with courage, we know that we have done something pleasing to you, God. Amen.

- *Is some amount of nervousness good for us when we take exams/tests?*

- *What is the best strategy to use when we begin to doubt ourselves and our answers?*

- *What is the source of our fears, and how can we ensure that our nerves do not take over?*

Excellence

For once you were darkness, but now in the Lord you are light.
Live as children of light. EPHESIANS 5:8

Our best is good enough

Dear God, we will always work to achieve excellence. We desire to do the very best we can do in all that we do. We fulfill the gifts you gave us when we work hard to exercise those gifts. We realize that there is nothing more important than every person working hard to maximize their potential. We pray to you to have the courage to strive for nothing less than excellence because you created excellence when you created us. Amen.

- *Do others expect us to do better than our best? If so, why?*

- *How do we know when we have done our best? How does it make us feel?*

- *Do other's opinions of our abilities help or hurt us as we strive to pursue our dreams?*

Let's give it our best

Dear God, help us to always strive for excellence. May we be able to give all we can to attain our personal best. Give us the eyes to see and the gift of prudence to recognize our achievements of excellence, despite the standards of the world. We also pray that we will be instruments for others, enabling and empowering them to be excellent. Amen.

- *What motivates us to always give our best?*

- *How can giving our best in school help other areas of our lives?*

- *What are the rewards of helping others attain excellence?*

Expectations

The desire of the righteous ends only in good; the expectation of the wicked in wrath. **PROVERBS 11:23**

I hate feeling like a disappointment

Dear Lord, we are not always capable of achieving that which is expected of us. There are times when we do let people down. We pray that others will understand that we do not want to let them down; rather, we simply could not fulfill what they have asked of us. Lord, help these people to understand and to be forgiving. Help them realize that although we may have not lived up to their expectations, we tried our best, and what we did offer is of great value. Amen.

- *What is the best way to respond when others expect too much of us?*

- *What should we do when people ask us for something we are not capable of doing?*

- *How might we help others see and appreciate when we are giving it our best?*

Reaching our potential

Dear Jesus, you expect us to be loving people, working to build the kingdom, loving and serving others. You have the expectation that we live up to our potential, working hard to actualize the gifts you have given us. There are times we will feel we have fallen short, but we know that you forgive us. You have expectations of us only because you know what great love we can bring to a broken world. Help us to reach our full potential, fulfilling your expectations and making the world a better place. Amen.

- *How can we come to know the expectations that God has for us?*

- *How can we best realize our full potential and meet these expectations?*

- *Should we feel any guilt or shame if we do not perform well in some areas? Why or why not?*

Faithfulness

Therefore, my beloved, be steadfast, immovable, always excelling
in the work of the Lord, knowing that in the Lord your labor is not in vain.
1 CORINTHIANS 15:58

A faithful people

Dear Lord, we pray that we will always remain faithful to our work and studies, to our friends and family, and to our call to follow you. Through being faithful and committed. We know that we are sure to succeed, bringing out the very best in ourselves and our loved ones and building your kingdom on earth. Be with us, Lord, especially through difficult and tempting times. May we see clearly, judge soundly, and always remain faithful to our promises and our calling. Amen.

- *How can we help those who may be finding it difficult to remain committed and faithful?*

- *What kinds of temptation prevent us from being committed?*

- *How can we mend a relationship broken because of a lack of faithfulness?*

Misguided faith

Dear Lord, at times we commit ourselves to people or groups that are destructive to ourselves and our community. We are lured by false promises and misled by promises of security and happiness. We ask you for the gift of prudence and self-discipline. Help us to discern between that which is unhealthy and harmful and that which will strengthen us and our community. Making a commitment and being faithful are important to our personal growth. Make us a committed and faithful people. Amen.

- *Why is being committed and faithful so important in our lives?*

- *Can things that provide us with comfort and peace be bad for us? Discuss.*

- *What can we do to help others break away from destructive commitments?*

Fairness

Remind them...to speak evil of no one, to avoid quarreling, to be gentle, and to show every courtesy to everyone. **TITUS 3:2**

Life is just not fair

Dear God, we don't understand why certain things happen in life. Bad things happen to good people, and good things happen to mean people. We often get mad and frustrated when we witness this. It is at these times that we need the ability to surrender, accepting the things we can't change, and not getting overwhelmed and angry. Grant us the faith to trust in you and to leave things in your hands. Amen.

- *Why do bad things happen to good people?*

- *Is it normal to get mad when you try to do everything right and something bad happens?*

- *What can we say to good people who have experienced bad things?*

Working to keep it fair

Dear Lord, help us to maintain fairness in all our dealings with others. May we be fair in our economic dealings, work relationships, friendships, and all other relationships. We are sometimes tempted to become angry or bitter, cold or crass, when life has not dealt us a fair hand. However, we pray that we can accept and forgive others and always maintain fairness in all that we do. As you said on the cross, "Forgive them; for they do not know what they are doing." Amen.

- *People were not fair with Jesus. How did he respond?*

- *How do we forgive someone who is not being fair to us or others?*

- *Does forgiving mean that we not act to make things right? Explain.*

Faith

"For truly I tell you, if you have faith the size of a mustard seed, you will say to this mountain, 'Move from here to there,' and it will move; and nothing will be impossible for you." **MATTHEW 17:20B**

Keep us faithful

Dear Lord, it is our faith in you that directs us, sustains us, and gives us life. As we progress through this school year, help us to make time to strengthen our faith. We make the effort to pray, to participate in the sacraments, and to gather as a community in your name. With our faith in you, we can overcome all obstacles, endure the difficult times, and find peace in all that we do. Amen.

- *How do we strengthen and develop our faith in today's world?*

- *How does our faith make our lives different?*

- *How do the liturgical seasons offer us an opportunity to develop our faith?*

Giving thanks for the gift of faith

Lord, we thank you for the gift of you and our faith in you. Our faith is such a blessing. Although there are times we doubt, question, and even abandon our faith, we always return to you. Our faith brings us comfort during the most difficult times, hope when all seems lost, and joy in the midst of sadness. So, thank you, Lord, for this wonderful gift of faith. Amen.

- *How and when does faith bring us comfort?*

- *Who are some people that we admire who have a strong and inspiring faith?*

- *Who are people in history whose faith guided and strengthened them?*

Family

"So when you are offering your gift at the altar, if you remember that your brother or sister has something against you, leave your gift there before the altar and go; first be reconciled to your brother or sister, and then come and offer your gift." MATTHEW 5:23-24

Help us get along

Dear Lord, we give you thanks for our families. However, sometimes it is difficult to get along with everyone in our homes. Give us the ability to always see their side so that we can appreciate the arguments that are being made. Give us the ability to walk in the shoes of other family members so we may be able to understand their arguments. In turn, Lord, we ask that you soften the hearts of our family members. May they too respect our opinions, listen to what we have to say, and be willing to compromise in order to reach decisions that are fair to all. Lord, bless our families and grant us the ability to get along, happily and successfully. Amen.

- *What are the important elements to ensure that families get along?*

- *Do some individuals have a greater tendency to fight? Why?*

- *How do some people behave differently at home as opposed to outside the home?*

We are appreciative of our families

God of light, we know that no family is perfect. We often take things for granted and place higher standards on our own family members. Help us to overcome any jealousies, conflicts, or bitter feelings that may get in the way of family harmony. May we always show pride in and appreciation for our family members. Help us to express the care and concern we truly have for one another. May our families be blessed with good health, joy, and love. Amen.

- *How do we show appreciation to our family members?*

- *What can we do to strengthen our familial relationships?*

- *What are some of the beautiful blessings that our family has given us?*

Finances

They are to do good, to be rich in good works, generous, and ready to share. 1 TIMOTHY 6:18

Share the wealth

Dear God, we know that many families in this community are struggling with financial problems. We pray that all people may be generous and help those in need. We never know when we will be the person who needs to ask for help. Many of these members in our society are brilliant and hardworking, but circumstances have gotten in the way of their financial prosperity. May we work hard to provide them with opportunity and relief. Amen.

- *Do we judge people who are struggling financially? If so, why?*

- *Is it possible for anyone to end up in a bad financial situation?*

- *Can someone be intelligent and hardworking and still experience financial difficulties?*

Money isn't everything

Dear Lord, it is a lifetime struggle to keep all things in perspective. We know that we need money to eat and purchase the basic necessities, but we are often misled by a society that is based on materialism and greed. We are led to believe that money will bring us happiness, and we get caught in a web of consumption. Keep our minds and hearts clear so that we may always see that it is not money that will bring us true happiness and that if we allow ourselves to get consumed in the grip of money, it can often lead to our demise. Amen.

- *Can money bring happiness?*

- *Can money bring unhappiness?*

- *What does bring happiness? Discuss.*

Flexibility

But God chose what is foolish in the world to shame the wise; God chose what is weak in the world to shame the strong. **1 CORINTHIANS 1:27**

Keep us open-minded

God, it is difficult to change our ways when we are convinced that we are right. Give us the humility to accept that we may be wrong and the prudence to know when we should be flexible in our thoughts and deeds. Help us to be more open to the ideas of others and celebrate their input and involvement. Give us the courage to admit when we are wrong and the strength to change our way of thinking. Amen.

- *Why is it so difficult to be flexible and to compromise?*

- *What are the advantages of being flexible in our work and personal lives?*

- *What are the consequences if people are never flexible or willing to compromise?*

Flexibility is our strength

Dear Lord, some view flexibility as a weakness. We ask the Holy Spirit to help us to discern so that we can recognize the times when flexibility is actually a strength and a sign of greatness. Flexibility is often a sign that we can see the other side of the argument, that we can understand another perspective, and that we are willing to work with others to make great things happen. We pray that our ego is always kept in check so that we can be flexible when we need to be and, in that flexibility, accomplish great things. Amen.

- *Is flexibility a strength or a weakness? Explain.*

- *How can we become more flexible?*

- *Can we become so flexible that others take advantage of us?*

Focus

This one thing I do: forgetting what lies behind and straining forward
to what lies ahead, I press on toward the goal for the prize.
PHILIPPIANS 3:13B–14

Getting back on track

Dear Lord, sometimes we are so busy doing school work, chores,
part-time jobs, sports, or maintaining a social life that we lose
focus. Help us to take time for prayer so that we can slow down
our pace and take time to focus and understand what we are being
called to do. Show us how to get our priorities straight so that we
can better serve you here on earth. Amen.

- *Is it difficult to change our priorities so that we can better focus
  on what is important?*

- *How do we know when we are off track? Can we be off track
  and be happy?*

- *Read the account of Martha and Mary in Luke 10:38–42.
  Discuss what Jesus' words to Martha mean to you.*

Help us stay focused

Dear Lord, it is not easy to remain focused. Our minds wander.
Our attention spans are short. We find it difficult to concentrate.

Help us to stay focused. It is our ability to completely focus on the project at hand that will lead to success. Grant us the skills we need to remain focused on what we are doing, to avoid being distracted and sidetracked. Amen.

- *Do some people have a harder time concentrating than others? Why?*

- *What are some things that cause us to lose focus?*

- *What are things that help keep us focused?*

Following Our Dreams

"You did not choose me but I chose you. And I appointed you to go and bear fruit, fruit that will last, so that the Father will give you whatever you ask him in my name." **JOHN 15:16**

Dream big!

Loving God, we love to dream big about our future. We love to be filled with excitement and enthusiasm about all the opportunities that lie before us. We pray today that we will have the confidence to know that no matter what our dream, we will be able to realize it, if we work hard at attaining it. We pray that we will be surrounded by supportive people who will offer us encouragement and praise and that we will make wise decisions that will provide us with the opportunities we need to help us reach our goals. God, we know that you want us to attain our dreams. Grant us the ability, confidence, and support to make it happen. Amen.

- *What are things that get in the way of attaining our dreams?*

- *Are youth encouraged to dream big?*

- *Do you think that youth believe they are capable of attaining their dreams?*

Reaching for the stars

Dear God, so many of your people were persecuted because they followed their dreams. They were viewed as different, odd, out of touch, and working outside of the box. Yet it was many of these very people who accomplished great things, changed the world, and made it a better place. Help us to stay true to the gifts you have given us. Give us the strength to follow our dreams and to never abandon what we believe you call us to do. Amen.

- *How does one feel when others look upon them and their actions as "odd" or "weird"?*

- *How do we overcome others who get in the way of fulfilling dreams?*

- *What role does faith play in attaining our dreams?*

Forgiveness

"You have heard it was said, 'An eye for an eye and a tooth for a tooth.' But I say to you, Do not resist an evildoer." MATTHEW 5:38–39

Let our forgiveness bring healing

Forgiving God, forgiveness is a powerful means of beginning the healing process. Help us to forgive those who have hurt us so that we may begin to heal our relationships. Help us to move beyond worldly limitations and experience and adopt your mercy and forgiveness. Through forgiving, we know that we will shed those destructive emotions of anger, hatred, and spite. May we be models of your love and forgiveness. Amen.

- *Does forgiveness help us with healing? Why or why not?*

- *When is forgiving most difficult?*

- *How can we become more forgiving persons?*

"Forgive them, Father"

Dear Jesus, it is not easy to forgive. We often become so hurt and angry over the actions of others that forgiveness seems like it is not an option. Help us, Jesus, to be able to forgive, no matter how difficult. May we think of your own passion and death. Even though others persecuted you, ridiculed you, spat on you, and humiliated you, your words before your death were "Father, forgive them; for they do not know what they are doing." May we be able to adopt your mercy and have the strength and faith to offer forgiveness to those who are in need of our forgiveness. Amen.

- *How was Jesus able to forgive those who humiliated and persecuted him?*

- *Do we change the heart of the person we forgive?*

- *Is it ever impossible to forgive?*

Friends

Let love be genuine; hate what is evil, hold fast to what is good; love one another with mutual affection; outdo one another in showing honor.

ROMANS 12:9–10

My friends are the best!

God of friendships, thank you for our friends. We're blessed to have great friends. They accept us as we are, help us when we are struggling, support us when we are down, and comfort us when we are sad. We pray that they know how grateful we are for their love and support. May we also be a great support to them through all their troubles. Amen.

- *Do we show our friends that we appreciate them? How do we show them?*

- *What are some of the obstacles that prevent us from meeting new friends?*

- *What are some factors that threaten relationships with friends?*

Who are my true friends?

God of friendships, it is not always easy to know whom we can truly count on. At times, our friends let us down or disappoint us. We know that none of us is perfect. Sometimes, however, we need help in determining whether we should be working on building friendships or simply moving on. We pray today for the wisdom to know and to recognize those people in our lives who are truly there for us, wanting to build us up and make us shine. May we be given the patience and forgiveness to be able to build upon these friendships and the strength to move on from those who are not good for us. Amen.

- *What makes someone a truly good friend? What characteristics do they possess?*

- *How can we offer friendship to those who are lonely and in need?*

- *Do friends sometimes "mess up"? Why? How should we respond when they do?*

Games/Sports

And not only that, but we also boast in our sufferings, knowing that suffering produces endurance, and endurance produces character, and character produces hope, and hope does not disappoint us, because God's love has been poured into our hearts through the Holy Spirit that has been given to us. **ROMANS 5:3–5**

Give it the best we've got! (game day)

Dear Lord, we have worked hard, individually and as a team, developing the gifts you have given us. Help us to play with respect yet be determined, to remain humble yet never doubt our ability, to play to our full potential yet always be sensitive to the needs of our own teammates. May all that we do show that we are athletes who are proud of, yet grateful for, our gifts. Be with us, Lord, and may we play a successful and injury-free game. Amen.

- *What are the elements that make us function best as a team?*

- *What is the key to success as a team?*

- *What can we do to assist everyone in this community to develop their talents?*

We like to win

Lord, we have practiced a great deal for this game. We pray that we will all give our personal best in today's game. Help us to be injury-free, respectful of the coaches and officials, and knowledgeable that our participation in this sport is something for which we are grateful. We have worked hard for this game, Lord, and we hope that our efforts will be reflected in our performance. Amen.

- *Is winning the most important thing in sports? If so, why? If not, what is?*

- *Can we learn anything from losing?*

- *Do we take for granted our ability to play sports? Does everyone get to play sports?*

Generosity

For during a severe ordeal of affliction, their abundant joy and their extreme poverty have overflowed in a wealth of generosity on their part. For, as I can testify, they voluntarily gave according to their means, and even beyond their means. **2 CORINTHIANS 8:2–3**

Blest be the giver

Most generous God, it is not always easy to give. We pray today for a willingness to demonstrate generosity. Help us to have the patience, time, and courage to step up when we are called upon.

May we be granted the love, compassion, and kindness that drive us to reach out to others. We pray for the wisdom, dedication, and skill to create initiatives that help others. Lord, may we never get tired of giving, knowing that in our generosity we will find peace and joy. Amen.

- *What do we find to be "life-giving" as opposed to "life-depleting"?*

- *Is "giving" energizing?*

- *In what ways can we be more sensitive to those around us?*

Keep us generous

Most generous God, you challenge us to be generous in all ways—to the poor with our financial resources; to our families with our time; to our friends, helping them through difficult times. Help us to be generous with our talents so that we can help build strong relationships; help us to be generous with all our gifts so that we can help build your kingdom. We pray for this spirit of generosity so that we can share with everyone all that we have to offer. Amen.

- *In what ways can we be generous with our gifts?*

- *How can we encourage others to be generous?*

- *In what ways does generosity enrich our own lives?*

Gentleness

Come to me, all you that are weary and are carrying heavy burdens, and I will give you rest." **MATTHEW 11:28**

Let's learn how to be gentle

Gentle Lord, there is not enough gentleness in our world. Our pace has become so fast and our lives so hectic that we often forget what gentleness means. Grant us the gift to be a gentle people and the ability to be gentle with those who are angry, with those who are hateful, and with those who suffer. May our words and actions always be an instrument of your gentleness. Amen.

- *When was Jesus gentle to those who may not have been deserving?*

- *What does gentleness mean? Do you experience it in your life? Where?*

- *How does a person develop this virtue and live it?*

Gentleness brings peace

Dear Jesus, when we read the gospels, we feel the gentleness that your presence provided. You gave each person your full attention in a loving and gentle manner. We know that when we are gentle, there is a calmness that brings peace. We have many people in our lives who are in need of our gentleness. Help us to be gentle to those around us, building relationships that are calming and founded on love. Amen.

- *Are there times when we know that gentleness is needed? If so, how do we know?*

- *Are there times when we should not be gentle? Discuss.*

- *Can gentleness be viewed as a weakness rather than a strength?*

Gifts

Like good stewards of the manifold grace of God, serve one another with whatever gift each of you has received. **1 PETER 4:10**

We are all talented

Dear God, we give thanks for the many blessings and gifts you have bestowed upon us. Help us to appreciate our own gifts as well as the gifts of others. May we work together to bring all that you have given us into beautiful harmony so that your majesty may be revealed in and through us. Amen.

- *Is every person gifted with a talent?*

- *Is it possible for individuals to go through their entire lives and not recognize their talent?*

- *Give examples of talents that we can use in our homes, parish, school, or community.*

We all have unique gifts

Dear Lord, you have granted unique gifts to each of us. Help us to recognize and appreciate these gifts in ourselves and in others. When we are able to do this, we know that we can attain great things together. By living out our gifts, we are fulfilling our purpose and coming closer to fulfilling our dreams. Grant us the confidence, insight, and patience to live out our gifts and help others live out theirs. Amen.

- *How do we discover our own gifts?*

- *How do we discover the gifts in others?*

- *Does society emphasize the value of some talents more than others? If so, which ones?*

Gossip

"Listen and understand: it is not what goes into the mouth that defiles a person, but it is what comes out of the mouth that defiles."
MATTHEW 15:10–11

Stop the gossip

Dear God, Pope Francis speaks about the destructive power of gossip and how it causes divisions in our lives and communities. We pray for the ability to look beyond what someone may say about us, and we pray that our words bring about unity and community. We pray for healing for those who cannot fight the temptation to gossip, and we pray that our words always bring about the goodness in others and create social harmony. Amen.

- *Why is gossiping such a strong temptation?*

- *In what ways are words of kindness more powerful than gossip?*

- *What techniques can we use to be more considerate in what we say about others?*

Gossip is ugly

Dear Lord, we hear and read gossip on the television, the Internet, in newspapers, and in everyday conversations. People tell stories about the personal lives and business of others. We call upon you to help all of us to overcome the temptation to gossip or say negative words about another. Give us a pure heart and mind so that the words we speak will build up your people, build up your creation, and build your kingdom on earth. Help us realize that it is kind and considerate words that demonstrate to others how good a person we are and that our words are pure and noble. Amen.

- *Is there is a lot of gossip in this community? If so, why?*

- *What are some of the things we can do to be more considerate and kind to others?*

- *How does our kindness toward others reflect and impact our own growth and lives?*

Grace

They are now justified by his grace as a gift, through the redemption that is in Christ Jesus. **ROMANS 3:24**

Grace power

Most gracious God, you offer us the gift of your grace. Help us to appreciate the power of your grace, to see that in and through your grace we are able to direct our lives in ways of faith. We may not be deserving, but because of your infinite love for us, you offer us your mercy and grace. It guides us and sustains us. Help us to

always keep an open heart and mind and always say "yes" to you,
O Lord. Amen.

- *What is God's grace? What can it do for us?*

- *What does it mean to accept God's grace?*

- *How does God's grace affect or change our lives?*

Grant them your grace, O Lord

Good and gracious God, there are many people who need to be
touched by your grace. They need to be strengthened in faith in
order for them to live to their full potential. As we now think
about these people, we ask that the blessing of your grace be
bestowed upon them. May the Holy Spirit guide them as they
transform their ways and receive conversion in and through your
grace. Amen.

- *Is there grace for the criminal, for those who have brought suffering
  to others?*

- *If there is grace for the undeserving, how can it change their lives?*

- *What are some ways that we can be an instrument of God's grace
  in the lives of others?*

Graduation

Before I formed you in the womb I knew you, and before you were born I
consecrated you. JEREMIAH 1:5

God bless our grads

Dear God, we pray for a special blessing for each of our graduates.

As they enter a new beginning, we pray that whichever path they choose will bring a sense of purpose and meaning. Help them to always use their gifts and talents in service to you, O Lord. May the world benefit from their gifts, and may they experience great joy in the sharing of these gifts. Amen.

- *How do we know what path to choose after graduation?*

- *What factors do we consider that can help us make decisions on the path we choose?*

- *Does everyone know what they want to do? What should they do if they have no idea?*

Today is our special day

Lord, today we give you thanks for the successful completion of our high-school experience. Many of our graduates and teachers have undertaken to make this celebration special. We give thanks for the wonderful years of friendships, gaining knowledge, and building a strong community, and for all the heartwarming memories. We pray that as we set out to fulfill our dreams, we will be granted confidence, direction, and discipline to fulfill all that we have imagined our lives to be. Amen.

- *Why do staff work so hard to provide a special celebration for the graduates?*

- *What makes this day meaningful? What do graduates look forward to the most?*

- *How can we show pride in the accomplishments of our colleagues on this special day?*

Gratitude

Make a joyful noise to the LORD, all the earth. Worship the LORD with gladness; come into his presence with singing. **PSALM 100:1-2**

Keep us grateful

Dear Lord, we recognize gratitude as the key attitude to happiness. It keeps us optimistic and appreciative. It feeds our heart, mind, and soul with the celebration of thanksgiving. This attitude of gratitude is pleasing to those around us and to you. May we see blessings in all our experiences, even those that bring suffering. In this way, Lord, we will be able to endure and overcome all things with a joy-filled heart. Amen.

- *Do we often take things for granted? If so, what types of things?*

- *What are ways in which we can adopt an attitude of gratitude?*

- *How does being grateful change the way we see things?*

Less is more

Dear Lord, it is interesting to see how many in the world do not have the basic necessities but do have a great deal of gratitude. They have barely enough food to feed themselves, yet they share what they have with others. They live in wooden shacks but invite their neighbors to come and live with them. They have little clothing but are willing to share what they have with others. We pray that we will have the same gratitude, joy of heart, and strong desire to share that our poorest of brothers and sisters show. Amen.

- *Can having too much take away an attitude of gratitude? If so, how?*

- *Are people with less more grateful than those with more?*

- *Why is it that we tend to appreciate things only after we lose them?*

Group Work

For we are God's servants, working together; you are God's field, God's building. **1 CORINTHIANS 3:9**

Let's share the work equally

Lord, group work sometimes presents problems. We pray that as we work on our class projects, each member of the group will take on an equal share of the work. At the same time, we pray that everyone remain sensitive to the strengths and weaknesses of our group members. Help us to work well together, to be open to each other's gifts, and to be respectful and appreciative of each other's contributions. Amen.

- *What should we do when someone is not doing their share of work in a group?*

- *How do we organize our work so that each person in the group is able to contribute their gifts?*

- *What are the characteristics of an effective group that accomplishes great things?*

Great things happen when we work together

Lord, today we work with others to accomplish a task. We pray for the gift of virtues: for humility so that we can remain open to the gifts of others; for generosity so that we can be of help to each other; for compromise so that we can accommodate each other's opinions; for courage so that we are not afraid to make our contributions; for compassion so that we can be of support to each other. Amen.

- *What are the ways in which we can get the most out of each member of our group?*

- *How do we bring out the gifts of those who are shy and less likely to speak up?*

- *Why are humility and compromise important ingredients to meeting with success?*

Happiness

"For those who want to save their life will lose it, and those who lose their life for my sake will find it." **MATTHEW 16:25**

Finding happiness

"[Happy] are the poor in spirit,
    for theirs is the kingdom of heaven.

[Happy] are those who mourn, for they will be comforted.

[Happy] are the meek, for they shall inherit the earth.

[Happy] are those who hunger and thirst for righteousness,
    for they will be filled.

[Happy] are the merciful, for they will receive mercy.

[Happy] are the pure in heart, for they will see God.

[Happy] are the peacemakers, for they will be called
children of God.

[Happy] are those who are persecuted for righteousness' sake,
for theirs is the kingdom of heaven." [**Matthew 5:3-10**]

- *How does society see these people—the mourners, the meek, etc.?*

- *Does society see the Beatitudes as the way to peace and happiness?*

- *Which Beatitude is the most difficult to put into practice? Why?*

Happiness, where are you?

Dear Lord, we all seek to be happy and yet it seems hard to
attain. We sometimes search for happiness in places that bring
pleasure, but all we end up with is misery. We sometimes seek
our happiness by trying to escape our suffering, and we find
emptiness. We pray for an open mind and an open heart so that
we will recognize where happiness truly lies. It is there, within us,
in the moment, given to us by you through your love and creation.
Amen.

- *Where do young people look for happiness?*

- *What brings people true happiness?*

- *Does being a servant to others, like Jesus, bring true happiness?*

Healing

When Jesus entered Peter's house, he saw his mother-in-law lying in bed with a fever; he touched her hand, and the fever left her, and she got up and began to serve him. **MATTHEW 8:14-15**

Born to make a difference

Good and loving God, help us not to get discouraged when we see the violence, wars, and poverty that afflict our world. You have bestowed upon us a multitude of talents that are meant to be developed and nurtured so that we may bring love and healing to the world. Just as you called Mahatma Gandhi, Martin Luther King Jr., and Nelson Mandela, you have called us to be healers. Through healing and elevating others, bringing them love and comfort, we will play an important part in building your kingdom of peace. Amen.

- *What qualities has God given us so that we can be healing agents in this world?*

- *Who are some popular people that are making a difference in their own way?*

- *If you could choose to overcome/fix/heal one thing in the world, what would it be?*

Lord, grant your healing touch

Dear Jesus, we give you thanks for the blessings and people who mean so much to us. Those who are always there for us, healing us when we are broken. Through them, you bring us your healing touch. Just as you healed the blind, the leper, the crippled, and the sinner, you heal us through these special people in our lives.

Thank you, Jesus, for the healing you brought to this world and for your continued acts of love and comfort through those special people in our lives. Amen.

- *Who are these people who bring healing into our lives?*

- *How can we be a healing presence in the lives of others?*

- *Jesus calls all of us to be healers. Who are the people in the greatest need of healing?*

Help

"Then the king will say to those at his right hand, 'Come, you that are blessed by my Father, inherit the kingdom prepared for you from the foundation of the world; for I was hungry and you gave me food, I was thirsty and you gave me something to drink'....Then the righteous will answer him, 'Lord, when was it that we saw you hungry and gave you food, or thirsty and gave you something to drink? And when was it that we saw you a stranger and welcomed you, or naked and gave you clothing? And when was it that we saw you sick or in prison and visited you?' And the king will answer them, 'Truly I tell you, just as you did it to one of the least of these who are members of my family, you did it to me.'"

MATTHEW 25:34–40

I need help...I don't get this work

Dear Jesus, it is not easy to ask for help. We feel like we are bothering people. We feel like we should understand but are unable to grasp the concepts. Help us to recognize that there are people who are happy to help us. Grant us a new vision so that we do not see ourselves as a bother but rather as a student and friend who needs a little extra explanation. We pray for the courage to ask the teacher or fellow classmates for help when we are in need. Amen.

- *Why are people hesitant to ask for help?*

- *Can we recognize people who need help even though they have not asked for it?*

- *Is asking for help sometimes viewed as a sign of weakness?*

I need someone I can trust

Dear God, we pray today that we are each blessed with people in our lives who can help us. We pray for the guidance of the Holy Spirit as we choose the right people to reach out to and confide in. May those we entrust with our problems understand the importance of confidentiality and work to help us through whatever issues we face. Amen.

- *Is it important to have at least one person in our life we can trust? Why?*

- *What happens to people when others break their trust?*

- *What are the qualities a trustworthy person should have?*

Helpfulness

Bear one another's burdens, and in this way you will fulfill the law of Christ.
GALATIANS 6:2

Everyone loves a joyful giver

Lord, may we always be willing to be helpful. When others are in need of our attention, may we always be willing to assist them. It is not always easy for people to ask for help, so we pray that we will be sensitive enough to see when others are in need of our help. May we be joyful givers who always find the time it takes to help others in need. Amen.

- *Why do we hesitate to help others?*

- *Are we able to be joyful when we are sacrificing for others?*

- *When we help others, does it inspire them to be helpful?*

Keep us helpful

Jesus, you walked the earth helping everyone. You helped the hungry by multiplying the loaves, the sick by curing their diseases, the oppressed by freeing them of their oppressor, and the suffering by ridding them of their afflictions. We pray for this spirit of helping others. There is nothing more comforting than to hear that someone wants to simply help. We pray that we can be like you, reaching out to help others and asking for nothing in return. Amen.

- *Do you think Jesus ever got tired of helping people?*

- *What attitude(s) do we need to adopt to be a person always helping others?*

- *How can we refuel ourselves when we feel exhausted from helping others?*

Heroes

"Either make the tree good, and its fruit good; or make the tree bad, and its fruit bad; for the tree is known by its fruit." **MATTHEW 12:33**

We all need heroes

Dear God, we pray for all those in our lives who serve as our heroes. We thank you for their beautiful gifts and for the inspiration they have instilled in us. Help us to follow their example and be inspired to do good. May we continue to be blessed with heroes, and may they in turn be rewarded for their goodness and kindness. Amen.

- *What are the qualities of a hero?*

- *Who are some modern-day heroes?*

- *In your own personal life, who is your hero?*

Make us heroes

Dear Jesus, you were a hero to the people but not because you were rich or famous or powerful. You were not a hero because you led an army, had celebrity status, or lived in a palace. You were a hero because of the nature of the man you were. Through your words and actions you offered love, forgiveness, hope, and peace. You stood up for what you believed to be true and were willing to suffer the consequences. You defended the weak, who could not defend themselves. We pray that we may emulate you in all that we do so that we might be heroes to others. Amen.

- *Who were some of the people Jesus was a hero to?*

- *We all have qualities that can make us heroic. What are the qualities of your hero?*

- *Are we faced with opportunities on a daily basis that enable us to be heroes? Discuss.*

Holy Spirit

"The Holy Spirit will teach you at that very hour what you ought to say."
LUKE 12:12

We need the Holy Spirit

Spirit of God, as we live each day, keep our hearts open to receiving you and all your gifts. When we struggle with decisions, help us to find wisdom. When we face difficult times, give us courage and strength. When we are faced with life-changing decisions, grace us with the understanding and prudence to make the right decisions. Holy Spirit, may our faith be strengthened daily—through prayer and spending quiet time with you. Amen.

- *What role does the Holy Spirit play in our lives?*

- *How do we discern that it is the Holy Spirit speaking to us?*

- *What are the gifts of the Holy Spirit? How do these gifts help us?*

Gifts of the Holy Spirit

Dear Lord, we know that we received the gifts of the Holy Spirit at the time of our confirmation. Today, we remind ourselves of these gifts: wisdom, understanding, counsel, fortitude, knowledge, piety, and fear of the Lord. May these gifts guide our lives. Lord, you bring yourself to us in every way, as Father, as Son, and as

Holy Spirit, so that we may understand the greatness of your love and the gift of yourself to all of creation. Amen.

- *How did you feel when you received the gifts of the Holy Spirit at your confirmation?*

- *Which is your favorite gift of the Holy Spirit? Why?*

- *Do you have different relationships with the three persons of the Trinity?*

Honesty

Therefore rid yourselves of all sordidness and rank growth of wickedness, and welcome with meekness the implanted word that has the power to save your souls. **JAMES 1:21**

Honesty is the best policy

Dear Lord, it is not easy to be honest. It is often much easier to lie in order to avoid trouble. Help us to always remain true to ourselves, to you, and to others. Grant us the discipline and courage to be honest. Help us to see that lying will only lead us down a path of more lies. Although it may be difficult at times, we pray that we never sacrifice our integrity and always retain our dignity. Amen.

- *Are there ever situations where it is acceptable to lie? If so, when and why?*

- *What characteristics does a person need to have to always be truthful?*

- *What are some of the consequences of living a dishonest life?*

Grant us the courage to be honest

Dear Jesus, when you were arrested and placed on trial it must
have been difficult for you to be honest. You knew that if you
answered honestly it meant your suffering and death. Throughout
your mission you were always honest, even when people did
not want to hear what you had to say because it challenged or
threatened them. It was your honesty that played a vital role in
changing the entire world, in all that people think, say, and do.
We pray for the courage to always be honest, to take responsibility
for our actions and our thoughts, and to play an active role in
changing the world. Amen.

- *If Jesus was dishonest and saved himself, how would the world
  be different today?*

- *What was it about Jesus' character that allowed him to always
  remain honest?*

- *As a school and a society, how can we encourage honesty in people?*

Honor Roll

We have gifts that differ according to the grace given to us: prophecy
in proportion to faith; ministry, in ministering; the teacher, in teaching;
the exhorter, in exhortation; the giver, in generosity; the leader, in diligence;
the compassionate, in cheerfulness. **ROMANS 12:6-8**

We made honor roll

Dear Lord, we give you thanks today for the ability to reach
our goal of attaining honor roll status. Thank you for the gift of
discipline, which helped us to study into those late-evening and

early-morning hours; for the gift of study partners, who helped us have a better understanding of the material; for our teachers, who worked hard to assist us to get the math formula, succeed on the science experiment, understand the religion lesson, and create the perfect paragraph. We pray that we will continue to develop our intellect to the best of our ability as we move forward toward fulfilling our dreams. Keep us forever grateful and hard working. Amen.

- *How does a person feel when they have actualized their gifts?*

- *Why is it that some students work very hard but cannot achieve honor roll status?*

- *Do we as a school community accept that everyone has different gifts? Give examples.*

Striving to make honor roll

Dear Lord, we pray to put forth our best this year. We have set a personal goal of making the honor roll. We know that not everyone can make this grade, for we all have different gifts. For those who work hard and whose gifts are in other areas, we pray for their success in the area in which they are most gifted. Some may not make the school honor roll, but because of their great character and excellence in other areas, they make *your* honor roll. Amen.

- *What are things that will help us put our best effort forward?*

- *Is attaining honor-roll status important? Why or why not?*

- *What does it mean to be on life's honor roll? Why is this more important?*

Hope

Keep your lives free from the love of money, and be content with what you have; for he has said, "I will never leave you or forsake you." **HEBREWS 13:5**

Taking up our cross

Lord of life and hope, thank you for the many blessings we have been granted. We take this time to remember that you have the power to breathe new life into those who are depressed, alone, and without hope. Help us to confront obstacles that prevent us from being fully alive and following you. Through your life, death, and resurrection, you breathe hope into our lives. We live in the knowledge that each day is a new day and that the future offers us endless opportunities. Amen.

- *When are times in which the youth experience hopelessness?*

- *Are some people given a heavier cross to bear in life? Why?*

- *What are some strategies that we can use when things get tough?*

In the cross there is victory

Dear God, it is with great joy and reverence that we celebrate the resurrection of our Lord Jesus Christ and the spiritual path he set for all of us to follow. We are filled with wonder and gratitude for the sacrifice that Jesus made for all of us. Your Son has set us free and shown us the way. No matter how difficult times are and the obstacles we must overcome, he has offered us hope. Through the knowledge that you are always with us, the hope that your Son offered us, and the love you give to us, we live our lives in hope. Amen.

- *What does this paradox mean: in sorrow there is joy; in defeat there is victory?*

- *What does it mean when we say that we are a people of hope?*

- *When have there been difficult times in society but hope pulled people through?*

Humility

"So whenever you give alms, do not sound a trumpet before you, as the hypocrites do in the synagogues and in the streets, so that they may be praised by others. Truly I tell you, they have received their reward. But when you give alms, do not let your left hand know what your right hand is doing." MATTHEW 6:2–3

Hooray for the humble of heart

Dear Lord, it is not always easy to be humble, particularly when we succeed at something. However, we know it is those who are humble who earn the respect, love, and appreciation of others around them. It is usually the most humble who excel. Grant each of us the gift of humility. Keep us mindful that all of our gifts and achievements are only made possible in and through your giving of those gifts to us. Amen.

- *Does society encourage us to be humble or to be boastful?*

- *How does one remain humble? What helps us to live with humility?*

- *Are humble people the people we admire the most?*

Humility is the best policy

Dear Lord, as we work hard to develop our gifts and accomplish great things, we pray that we will always remain modest. People do not appreciate others when they are boastful or conceited. As we become the wonderful people you have created us to be, may we do it with modesty and humility. We pray that we will never get wrapped up in ourselves, allowing our ego to get in the way of the good work we are called to do. Amen.

- *How does it make us feel when people act conceited? Do we think more or less of them?*

- *What does it mean to be humble? How do we ensure that we always remain humble?*

- *Was Jesus humble? Give examples from his life.*

Illness

Great crowds came to him, bringing with them the lame, the maimed, the blind, the mute, and many others. They put them at his feet, and he cured them, so that the crowd was amazed when they saw the mute speaking, the maimed whole, the lame walking, and the blind seeing. And they praised the God of Israel. MATTHEW 15:30-31

Heal them, Lord

Healing God, today we pray for all those who are ill. We each know of someone who is in need of healing, and we bring them to mind at this time. *(pause)* We pray that they find comfort and hope through your love, and strength through the love of family and friends. We pray for their healing of body and spirit. Amen.

- *Why do some people get struck with illness and others do not?*

- *What can we do to bring comfort and consolation to those who are ill?*

- *What can we learn from suffering and illness?*

Please call them home, Lord

God of love and comfort, it is very difficult to see our loved ones suffer. We often wish that we could bear the suffering for them. We pray for *(name of person)* today. We know that they are close to death and are suffering. We ask you, Lord, to embrace them with your love and be with them when you call them home. We find some comfort in knowing they will share in your glory, where they will be at peace and eternal rest. Amen.

- *How do we feel when a loved one is suffering? Is it normal to feel anger?*

- *What can we do to help others who are dealing with a family member who is suffering?*

- *In what ways can suffering make us greater people?*

Integrity

But now you must get rid of all such things—anger, wrath, malice, slander, and abusive language from your mouth. Do not lie to one another, seeing that you have stripped off the old self with its practices and have clothed yourselves with the new self, which is being renewed in knowledge according to the image of its creator. **COLOSSIANS 3:8–10**

We are in charge of who we are

Dear Lord, there are many things that people can say about us that are not true. There are many rumors that people can spread that we cannot stop. There are many stories that people make up that never happened. You have taught us that the best way to counter these incidents is to be authentic and moral. Grant us the wisdom to respond in ways that help reveal who we truly are. Grant us the strength to never get caught up in falsehoods, but rather to focus on truth. Grant us the confidence to recognize that the truth does in fact set us free. We know, Lord, that in the end, it is between you and us. Amen.

- *Why do people start rumors about others? Do they recognize how malicious they are?*

- *Is it tempting to fall into this dialogue and also spread rumors?*

- *What does it mean to never sacrifice our integrity?*

Keep us on the right track

Lord, we do not always know what to do. Sometimes we are put into situations where we do not know what to say or how to respond. Help us in these situations to say and do things that are pleasing to you, O Lord. We pray that the words we speak may empower others to be great people. We know that if we follow your way, we will never compromise our integrity, and we will live a moral life filled with peace and joy. Amen.

- *What does the word integrity mean?*

- *How do we know what an effective but proper response is to gossip and rumors?*

- *How can we better understand how God wishes us to respond?*

Jesus

Then Jesus said to the Jews who had believed in him, "If you continue in my word, you are truly my disciples; and you will know the truth and the truth will make you free." JOHN 8:31

Jesus is with us

A reading from the holy Gospel according to Luke: "[While the disciples were talking,] Jesus himself stood among them and said to them, 'Peace be with you.' They were startled and terrified, and thought that they were seeing a ghost. He said to them, 'Why are you frightened, and why do doubts arise in your hearts? Look at my hands and my feet; see that it is I myself. Touch me and see; for a ghost does not have flesh and bones as you see that I have.' And when he had said this, he showed them his hands and his feet. While in their joy they were disbelieving and still wondering, he said to them, 'Have you anything here to eat?' They gave him a piece of broiled fish, and he took it and ate in their presence."

[LUKE 24:35-48]

- *What does this Scripture passage mean?*

- *We are told: "I can do all things through Christ who strengthens me." What does this mean?*

- *How can we be sure that when we do things, they are what Jesus wants us to do?*

Jesus helps us overcome

Dear Jesus, you demonstrated that even in the depths of despair, pain, and suffering you never abandoned your mission or your message. Help us, particularly those who are struggling with sadness, illness, or loneliness, to feel your presence and your love. Give us the courage to fulfill our mission, even in the depths of despair and suffering. May we each walk with you and remember that we are a joy-filled people and "alleluia" is our song. Amen.

- *What are some ways in which we can overcome difficult times?*

- *What can we do to be more optimistic about our lives?*

- *How does Jesus help us to get through troubled times and fulfill our mission?*

Job

My brothers and sisters, whenever you face trials of any kind, consider it nothing but joy, because you know that the testing of your faith produces endurance. JAMES 1:2–4

Wealth is in the person, not the money

Dear God, many people suffer as a result of losing their job. May they recognize that their greatness is not measured by the job they have but by how much they love others and how much they have done to help others. Grant all those who are jobless a sense of dignity and confidence and the realization that their worth is not measured by material gain. Amen.

- *Do you think God will be more interested in the jobs we held or the people we helped?*

- *Does society measure a person's worth and success through the jobs people hold?*

- *What is the true test of a successful person?*

I need a job

Dear Lord, many of us need part-time jobs. Help us, Lord, to secure employment so that we may help our families and save money for our future education. Impart wisdom to our politicians and business people so that they will work to create a society with job opportunity and prosperity. We pray that they will not be ruled by greed and profits but by doing what is best for the whole of society. Amen.

- *Is working a part-time job while in school good for young people? Explain.*

- *Is having a job a basic human right?*

- *Do the rights of the people to have work motivate big business, or does profit alone?*

Joyfulness

I am filled with consolation; I am overjoyed in all our affliction.

2 CORINTHIANS 7:4B

Be happy

God of joy, we are often tempted to be miserable and find comfort in being negative. Yet joy is such a wonderful gift and a beautiful state of mind. We experience joy in the birth of a child, the marriage of a couple, and the graduation of a student. We pray that we will always be joy-filled people and that the joy we experience throughout our day will make others feel happy and positive. Amen.

- *What does it mean to be joyful?*

- *Are people generally joyful? Is it difficult to be joyful?*

- *Why are some people always filled with joy and others always sad?*

Keep us optimistic

Dear Lord, it is not always easy to be optimistic. There is always something in our lives that is difficult to overcome. Help us, even in our most difficult times, to always remain optimistic. We know that when we approach our tasks and obstacles with optimism and joy, things are a great deal easier. Help us, Lord, to always see the light, to focus on the stars, and to stay out of the mud. Amen.

- *How can we remain optimistic in difficult times?*

- *How does optimism shape our future endeavors and careers?*

■ *Who are some successful people who are optimistic and always joy-filled?*

Judging

"Do not judge, so that you may not be judged. For with the judgment you make you will be judged, and the measure you give will be the measure you get." **MATTHEW 7:1–2**

Stop the judging

Merciful God, you challenge us not to judge. It may be because when we judge we hurt others. It may be because we hurt our own spiritual development. Open our hearts and our minds so that we realize judging others is destructive to them and to our own well-being. Keep us positive and help us to focus on ways we can improve our own lives, as opposed to ways others should improve. Amen.

■ *Why do we judge others?*

■ *How does it make us feel when we judge others?*

■ *How does it hurt our own spiritual and psychological development?*

Who is the judge?

Dear Lord, we know it is not our place to judge. We are often wrong when we judge others. We often form opinions that result in us changing our behavior and acting differently. Our judging can influence others in negative ways. We do not walk in the shoes and live the life of another person. Help us to remember that it is you who are the ultimate judge. When we die, we will stand before you, and no one else. Amen.

- *Does judging another person make one feel empowered or better than that person?*

- *What is the difference between judging actions and judging a person?*

- *How can we prevent others from judging? How can we prevent ourselves from judging?*

Justice

And what does the Lord require of you but to do justice, and to love kindness, and to walk humbly with your God. MICAH 6:8

Let's change the world

God of justice, there are many things in the world that do not seem fair. Food is thrown away while people die of starvation. Wars are started for profit. Water is polluted and wasted while millions go thirsty and die from unclean lakes and rivers. Strengthen and enlighten us so we may be instruments of justice. Amen.

- *Is it humans or nature that causes the injustice and unfairness in the world?*

- *What are some examples of injustice and unfairness?*

- *What can we do individually and as a school to be instruments of justice?*

Let justice prevail

Dear Lord, help us to be creators of justice. When things do not seem right, give us the courage to step up and take a stand. When we witness acts that humiliate others, help us to bring dignity back to the person. When we hear things that are destructive and hurtful, help us to use the right words to bring peace and healing. Lord, help us to be instruments of your peace so that we may attain justice for all. Amen.

- *What does justice mean?*

- *What are some examples of injustice in the world?*

- *Is justice something important enough to make great sacrifices to attain?*

Kindness

As God's chosen ones, holy and beloved, clothe yourselves with compassion, kindness, humility, meekness, and patience. **COLOSSIANS 3:12**

Bring on the kindness

God of kindness, we know that in each of us there is a kind and gentle spirit. We know this because we have been created in your image. Help us to develop this gift of kindness. May our example and our efforts encourage others to be kind. If we were all kind to each other, we would live in a different world. It would be a world that comforts people and helps them through the most difficult times. It would truly reflect your kingdom. Amen.

- *What does it mean to be kind? How would you define "kind"?*

- *What are the obstacles that we face that make it difficult to be kind?*

- *Do we feel better or worse when we perform kind acts?*

Let us lead by example

God of all, we know that acts of kindness bring smiles to faces. Whether we have someone opening a door for us or helping us with our homework or taking our shift at work, or buying us a gift, these acts of kindness are life-giving and bring great joy. In a world that is often focusing on the negative, help us to change that and to bring out the positive. Help us to be kind so that we may bring peace and joy to others. Amen.

- *Why would some people view kindness as a weakness?*

- *How does it change a person when someone is kind to them?*

- *Name an extraordinarily kind person.*

Life Is Sacred

See what love the Father has given us, that we should be called children of God; and that is what we are. The reason the world does not know us is that it did not know him. **1 JOHN 3:1**

Life is sacred. Stop the abuse

God of love and life, we know that we have been made in your image. When we look around us, we see and witness acts of people who do not appreciate the dignity of the person. We see people abused, bullied, and traumatized by others. Help us to have the courage to put an end to this and to be able to help people recognize their God-like nature. Help us through our own actions to demonstrate that we are all God-like and need to live this way every day of our lives. Help us to ensure that all people and all human life is respected. Amen.

- *Does our society view some people as better than others? If so, what are the criteria?*

- *What groups of people are not viewed as equal or sacred?*

- *What can we do to guarantee that all people are treated as sacred?*

We choose life

God of love, we understand that carrying a child to full term and giving birth may sometimes be difficult. Some women, particularly those who are single and still in high school, face rejection by their parents, embarrassment in the community, and distancing from their friends. We pray for all these women today. May they be granted the support that enables them to have their babies and to recognize the gift of life that is within them. May they be confident in their own strengths, and may this lead to healthy deliveries and happy lives. Amen.

- *How does this community respond to students who get pregnant? Is the response fair?*

- *What can we do to help pregnant students carry their babies to full term?*

- *What support can we offer single pregnant women that would be helpful to them?*

Loneliness

Then he said to them, "I am deeply grieved, even to death; remain here, and stay awake with me." **MATTHEW 26:38**

May we never feel alone

Dear Lord, although we are surrounded by people, sometimes we feel alone. It does not matter how many times the phone rings for us, how many text messages we get a day, or how many people are inviting us to hang out, we can still feel alone. Help us to know that there is a place in this world for us. Help us to come to understand the service for which you created us. Help us to always know and feel your presence so that we never feel completely alone. Lord, we know that you know us and understand us better than we know ourselves. Amen.

- *Is it possible for a person to have a lot of friends and still feel lonely?*

- *How do feelings of loneliness come about?*

- *What can we do for people who feel lonely?*

Let's visit

God of all, many people do not have family and friends. They are often alone and do not have the ability to share things with others. Some of these people are homeless, some are in our retirement homes, nursing homes, and mental health facilities, and some are here among us. Help us, Lord, to do what we can to let these people know that they are not alone. Help us to model the example of Saint Teresa of Calcutta, who worked tirelessly to ensure that each and every person was not alone. May we be your witness to the lonely, bringing to them your comfort and love. Amen.

- *Why do we have so many lonely people in our community?*

- *Why is it with all our social media, there are so many lonely teens?*

- *How did Saint Teresa bring comfort to those who were lonely?*

Love

Love is patient; love is kind; love is not envious or boastful or arrogant or rude. It does not insist on its own way; it is not irritable or resentful; it does not rejoice in wrongdoing, but rejoices in the truth.

1 CORINTHIANS 13:4–6

Share the love

God of love and light, love is the greatest of gifts. We witness great love in the world— parents' love for their child, a fiancé's love for their partner, a missionary's love for the poor, the love you showed by dying for our sins. We pray today that we may be creators of love. We know that you have said to us, "no one has greater love than this, to lay down one's life for one's friend." Help us, Lord, to be a beacon of light and love in the life of others. Amen.

- *What would the world be like if everyone loved one another?*

- *Do we allow our problems to get in the way of loving others?*

- *How did Jesus demonstrate his love to the world? Did it transform or change people?*

Love God and love your neighbor

Dear Jesus, you summed up the Ten Commandments with the

two great commandments: "Love the Lord your God with all your heart...and your neighbor as yourself." May we be open to the Holy Spirit so that we may always choose the way of love. As difficult as it may be at times, we know that the path of love that you carved is the path for us to walk. Help us to be strengthened in faith so that we make decisions that are faithful to the life to which you call us. Amen.

- *Are we capable of loving the way Jesus calls us to love?*

- *What does it mean to "love your neighbor as yourself"?*

- *Why did Jesus sum up the Ten Commandments into the two commandments cited above?*

Loyalty/Trustworthiness

A poor widow came and put in two small copper coins, which are worth a penny. Then he called his disciples and said to them, "Truly I tell you, this poor widow has put in more than all those who are contributing to the treasury. For all of them have contributed out of their abundance; but she out of her poverty has put in everything she had, all she had to live on." **MARK 12:42–44**

Help me be trustworthy

Dear Lord, we know how friends rely on us and trust in us. Today we pray that we will not disappoint our friends. May we stay on track and fulfill our promises to them. At times it will be inconvenient and difficult to remain faithful, but we pray for the determination and perseverance to live up to the promises we make. Amen.

- *What are things that get in the way of fulfilling our promises?*

- *What are the ways in which we can find the strength to remain trustworthy and loyal?*

- *Are there times when it is unwise to keep our promises? When?*

Strength during disappointment

Dear Lord, it is not easy to trust. Sometimes people let us down. You know this, Lord, because one of your own disciples betrayed you. Give us the virtue of forgiveness, and help us to move forward whenever we have been betrayed. Be with us so that we do not allow it to take away from the good people in our lives. Amen.

- *How do we overcome disappointment from others?*

- *How do we not let disappointment make us bitter or distrusting?*

- *Did Jesus become bitter or unforgiving when he was betrayed?*

Mary

[And the Angel Gabriel came to Mary] and said, "Greetings, favored one! The Lord is with you." **LUKE 1:28**

Mary struggled too!

Dear Mary, it was through your courage and faith that you were able to accept God's plan. Your life was not an easy one as you faced ridicule and hardship. You had the strength and courage to rise above all of this. Your faith enabled you to put all those who made hurtful claims behind you, and you always kept God in front of you. We pray today for this kind of faithfulness. Mary, we ask for your intercession to enable us to live a life that is faithful and meaningful. May the example that you gave us inspire and direct us as we too attempt to accept God's call and God's love. Amen.

- *What were some of the difficulties that Mary faced?*

- *How was she was able to overcome them?*

- *What traits of Mary should we pray to have?*

Your example rocks!

Dear Mary, we look to your life and your love as an inspiration and guide. We pray that each of us may be blessed with the faith that enables us to respond to God's call to be humble and faithful servants, like you. We pray for the perseverance, determination, love, and ability to accept all that God wills for us. We ask that you pray for us, that we may attain these qualities. Amen.

- *How was Mary able to put her faith first in everything she did?*

- *How can we become more surrendering, accepting God's will?*

- *If our faith came first, in what ways would this change the people we are?*

Meaning (To Find)

"What will it profit them if they gain the whole world but forfeit their life?"

MATTHEW 16:26

May the Holy Spirit be with us

Dear Holy Spirit, as we progress through this semester, we reflect on our lives. We pray that, with your guidance, we will be able to find meaning and purpose. We all have a meaning and purpose to live for, but sometimes it is hard to find. We pray that we can shake those feelings that confuse us and see more clearly our purpose and meaning, and that, with your love, we can live out that purpose. Amen.

- *What does it mean to be clear-minded and open to God's call?*

- *When people are confused, what can they do to discover their meaning and purpose?*

- *How do we know when we are following the way of the Holy Spirit?*

Guide us, Holy Spirit

Dear God, what am I to do in my life? What am I to become? What path am I supposed to take? How do I live life to the fullest? These, O Lord, are questions we ask ourselves. We pray today for the direction of the Holy Spirit to assist us in making decisions that lead to living full and meaningful lives. May we choose the path that leads to the greatest result, and may we have confidence as we walk that path. Amen.

- *What resources are available to us to help us make good decisions about our future?*

- *Do we know when we are making a bad decision? If so, how do we change direction?*

- *Can you name great people who changed direction many times to find their purpose?*

Media/Technology

Then Jesus said to the Jews who had believed in him, "If you continue in my word, you are truly my disciples; and you will know the truth, and the truth will make you free." JOHN 8:31–32

Let's not get sucked in

Dear Lord, we see many advertisements on billboards, on television, and on our computers. Some are upsetting, and many are misleading. Give us the discernment to distinguish between that which is true and good and that which is false and destructive. May we have the strength and the intellect to never allow the media or anyone to take us away from you. Amen.

- *Do the media promote values that are dangerous? If so, which values?*

- *Do the media provide positive messages that promote gospel values?*

- *Are people able to see through the marketing and recognize truth or falsity?*

Media/technology can be exciting

Lord, there are so many advancements in technology. We are grateful for the new and exciting options available to us. We pray that we may use our technological skills to create an even more technologically advanced world. And we pray that whatever we create is always for the good of humanity, creating a healthier, safer, and freer world. Amen.

- *When the media say something is good and cool, is it really good and cool or just a sales pitch?*

- *Are technological advancements positive? Are there any dangers?*

- *What kinds of technological advancements are creating a better world?*

Mental Health

Blessed be the God and Father our Lord Jesus Christ, the Father of mercies and the God of all consolation, who consoles us in all our affliction, so that we may be able to console those who are in any affliction with the consolation which we ourselves are consoled by God. **2 CORINTHIANS 1:3–4**

It is not their fault

Dear Lord, there are many in our community and our society who suffer mental health issues. We know that these issues can affect people of all ages. Today we pray for healing for all those who are suffering from mental health issues. We pray that as a society we will pay more attention to this concern, be more sensitive to their needs, and create programs to help them. May they be granted peace in their time of turmoil, comfort in their time of distress, and calm in their time of anxiety. Bless them, Lord, and be with them. Amen.

- *Do we fully understand mental illness?*

- *How do we treat people with mental illness?*

- *Why do some with mental illness take their own lives?*

Modesty

Live in harmony with one another; do not be haughty, but associate with the lowly; do not claim to be wiser than you are. **ROMANS 12:16**

Let honesty prevail

God, you have gifted us with talents and skills. May we always realize that all the gifts we have come from you. Although we need to develop and nurture these gifts, you are their source. Help us, no matter how much we succeed, to remain modest and humble. It is with modesty that we will accomplish so much more. Greatness is born from humility, and people love to be around those who are modest. Amen.

- *How does being modest influence those around us?*

- *How do we remain modest? Is it natural or do we have to work at it?*

- *What does modesty enable us to do that we would not be able to do if we were boastful?*

Keep us grounded

Dear Lord, you created all of us equal. No person is above or below another. May we never see ourselves as better than others. When we acknowledge that we are equal, we are more willing to reach out and help one another. We are more willing to work as a team with others. We will be more democratic in our dealings with others. Keep us grounded and loving. Keep us compassionate and kind. Amen.

- *Do we view others as our equals? Discuss.*

- *How can we become more loving, kind, compassionate, and generous people?*

- *How can we encourage people who are conceited to be more humble?*

Natural Disasters

"When you hear of wars and rumors of wars, do not be alarmed; this must take place, but the end is still to come. For nation will rise against nation, and kingdom against kingdom; there will be earthquakes in various places; there will be famines. This is but the beginning of the birth pangs."
MARK 13:7–8

Help them, Lord

Dear Lord, we are very saddened by the news of *(name the disaster)*. We will never understand, in this life, why these things happen. We only know that when they do happen we are saddened and confused, sometimes feeling helpless. We pray to you, Lord, for understanding, acceptance, and the ability to move forward to help the victims. May they know that people around the world are thinking about them and praying for them. May this help them to find comfort during this very difficult time. Amen.

- *Are we sympathetic and responsive to natural disasters around the world?*

- *How do people impacted by disaster deal with the devastation that they experience?*

- *Do we live in fear that a disaster could happen in our community/ city? If so, what type?*

What can we do?

Dear God, we pray today for all those who have been impacted by *(name the disaster)*. We pray that the Holy Spirit may guide us in ways to offer support to those who are suffering. May the response from this community be generous and thoughtful. May those who are struggling know that our thoughts and prayers are with them. May they find some comfort in knowing that we are there for them. May all our efforts offer healing and comfort. Amen.

- *Is offering prayer and well wishes enough support to the victims of natural disaster?*

- *What else can we do to lend support to those impacted by disaster?*

- *How do we motivate the school community to get involved?*

New Semester

For surely I know the plans I have for you, says the Lord, plans for your welfare and not for harm, to give you a future with hope. **JEREMIAH 29:11**

Let's work together

Lord, we pray for a year of good health and success. May we each grow and develop in mind, body, and spirit. May we be granted the wisdom to maintain the proper balance in life and the prudence to make significant contributions to this community. May we always be willing to make sacrifices that enable others to grow and that lead to the flourishing of this community. Lord, keep us humble and grateful as we strive to give our best to pave the way for a wonderful future. Amen.

- *What attitude can we adopt to help us perform to the best of our abilities?*

- *What are some of the things we can do to be "a person for others"?*

- *In what ways are we empowered to do great things when we feel the presence of God?*

Striving to be the best we can be

Good and gracious God, as we begin this school year, we pray that we may feel your presence and that it provide us with a source of comfort and strength. May all those who are new to this community feel welcomed and continuously encouraged to be themselves, sharing their gifts and talents in abundance. For those who are returning, may they continue to grow in wisdom, faith, and love. May their confidence in themselves and their abilities lead to a further enhancement of this great school community. God, we pray that this year will be one to remember. Fill it with happiness, growth, peace, and good health. Let all of our efforts and good works reflect the love, acceptance, and kindness that Jesus showed to us. We ask this through your Son, our Savior and friend. Amen.

- *What can we do as individuals and as a class to ensure this school year is a great one?*

- *What can we do to help those who are new to this community to feel welcomed?*

- *What can we do to remain true to the intentions we had at the beginning of the semester?*

New Student

The cup of the blessing that we bless, is it not a sharing in the blood of Christ? The bread that we break, is it not a sharing in the body of Christ? Because there is one bread, we who are many are one body, for we all partake of the one bread. **1 CORINTHIANS 10:16–17**

Let us welcome our new student

God of friendships, today we welcome (*name of new student*) into our classroom and our school. May the community offer a warm welcome and encourage (*name of student*) as he/she starts this new beginning. Help us to be willing to go out of our way to ensure that (*name of student*) has someone to eat lunch with, someone to chill with, and someone to do homework with. Grant to him/her warm and wonderful friendships. May our warmth and welcome assist him/her to attain great success and to be comfortable and happy in this environment. Amen.

- *What are some of the difficulties people experience when they move to a new community?*

- *What are some of the thoughts, fears, and feelings of a new student?*

- *What are ways that we can help students in this community feel welcomed?*

It is tough being the new student

Dear God, changing schools and being the new student is very difficult. Leaving friends behind and starting all over has its challenges. Help all of us to offer all new students a warm welcome. Help us to be there for them, to offer them company and support. May we put ourselves in their position and understand how they feel so that we may offer the help and direction they need. May all of our new students enjoy their time here, and may we help make this transition an awesome one. Amen.

- *Why are some people reluctant to make friends with a new student?*

- *Should we have a special orientation or program for new students?*

- *Do new teachers experience some of the same fears and apprehensions?*

New Year

O Lord, you have searched me and known me. You know when I sit down and when I rise up; you discern my thoughts from far away. **PSALM 139:1–2**

Let faith prevail

Dear Lord, as we begin this new year, we look upon it as a new beginning. We know that there are areas of our lives that we can improve upon. Help us to take time to reflect on how we can do this and live out our commitment to follow you. Grant us the discipline to follow through the commitments we make as a result of our reflection. When we face times of difficulty in fulfilling our commitments, may we know that you are there to carry us. Grant us the faith to ask for your help and for the willingness to be carried. Amen.

- *How can we ensure that faith remains a priority in our lives?*

- *What are things that get in the way of our faith?*

- *Why do our new year's resolutions often fade away quickly?*

Jesus is waiting to hear from us

Dear Jesus, as we begin this new year, help us to make it a priority to come to know you better. May we be willing each day to spend time with you, to talk to you, and to walk with you. May we be willing to surrender ourselves to you. Help us, Jesus, this year to be your faithful servants. May all we do be done for you. Amen.

- *Do we take enough time to talk to Jesus? If not, why?*

- *Do we know what to say when we talk to Jesus?*

- *If someone didn't know how to talk to Jesus, how should we direct them?*

Obedience

If we live by the Spirit, let us also be guided by the Spirit. GALATIANS 5:25

We don't like rules

Dear Lord, as teenagers we face rules every day. We have rules that our parents establish, rules that the school sets, and rules that society creates. Sometimes we feel that these rules limit who we are and what we can become. Help us to be respectful of the rules, yet when we need to challenge rules, fill us with the words to express our opinions respectfully and convincingly. Lord, help us to tolerate and abide by the rules that help us and to stand up to help change the rules that inhibit us. Amen.

- *What rules in our school are unfair and limiting?*

- *What rules in our school are helpful and necessary?*

- *How can we respectfully work to change rules that we do not agree with?*

Obedient to the end

Dear Jesus, you accepted the will of your Father and were obedient to the end. Help us to try to follow your example. It is not always easy to give up our own way of doing things in an effort to follow your will. We pray today for a better understanding of what you call us to do. We also pray for the strength to follow your way. Amen.

- *How do we know what God asks of us?*

- *How can we come to better understand the will of God?*

- *What characteristics are most important to be obedient to God's will?*

Opportunities

Be careful then how you live, not as unwise people but as wise.
EPHESIANS 5:15

Fill us with opportunities

Lord, each day we are presented with different opportunities. We do not always know which opportunities we should seize and which we should let go. Help us to remain open to the Spirit so that we may recognize opportunities that come our way that will benefit us and society.

Keep us open to your call so that we may always be willing to accept opportunities that will bring out the best in us. Amen.

- *Are there a lot of opportunities for young people? Why or why not?*

- *How do people receive opportunities? Do we sometimes miss opportunities?*

- *How do we know which opportunities we should pursue and which we should not?*

Grant us plenty of opportunities

Dear Lord, each of us has been blessed with unique gifts. Sometimes we can go through life and not know our own gifts. We pray today that our lives may be filled with opportunities that help us discover and exercise our gifts. Keep us brave and open to exploring different opportunities. Grant us an open mind and an open heart as we work to discover the wonderful gifts and opportunities with which we have been blessed. Amen.

- *Do some people have gifts that they fail to discover?*

- *How can a person come to discover their gifts?*

- *Does discovering gifts require a person to take risks and think outside the box?*

Optimism

I give thanks to my God always for you because of the grace of God that has been given you in Christ Jesus, for in every way you have been enriched in him, in speech and knowledge of every kind. **1 CORINTHIANS 1:4–5**

Smile! Be happy!

Dear God, help us to be aware of your awesome nature, which surrounds us. Keep us mindful of your goodness, kindness, and healing power. May we know that you are always there for us, to guide us, help us, and encourage us. With this knowledge, we will always be optimistic. Give us strength in times of trials, joy in times of success, patience in times of difficulty, and friendship in times of loneliness. Keep us optimistic, Lord, as we journey through life. Amen.

- *What is the secret to remaining optimistic?*

- *Does a positive attitude change what happens in a person's life?*

- *Is it possible to be optimistic when things really don't go our way? If so, how?*

Attitude is everything

Dear Lord, we know that when we have a positive attitude, the world seems like a better place. When we approach activities with an optimistic attitude, we are more likely to succeed. Lord, we pray today that no matter how tough our day, we will remain optimistic. When everything seems to be going wrong, we will remain optimistic and view it as a learning experience. We will be an inspiration to those around us when we remain optimistic even when everything seems to be going wrong. Amen.

- *Can a person remain optimistic no matter how many things go wrong in their life?*

- *Is being optimistic linked to what is going in one's life or is it an attitude?*

- *Do people who are optimistic tend to have better friendships?*

Parents

Children, obey your parents in the Lord, for this is right.
"Honor your father and mother." **EPHESIANS 6:1–2**

We love you, Mom and Dad

Lord , we give thanks for our parents. We know that we do not always act in ways that demonstrate the love we have for our parents, and we pray that we may become better at that. We are grateful for the blessing of our parents. We are grateful for their love, dedication, and commitment to doing everything to ensure that our life is the best it can be. Lord, may our parents know our love and gratitude for all they do, and may they be blessed for their endless efforts for us. Amen.

- *Why is it sometimes difficult to show our appreciation to our parents?*

- *Are parents aware of the love their children have for them?*

- *What can we do to better express our gratitude to our parents?*

We need healing

Dear God, we have not all been blessed with great parents. Some people struggle with parents who do not understand their children, make no time for them, or simply are more concerned with their own lives. We pray today for these parents and their children. May parents recognize the wonderful gift that their children are to them, and may they know that true happiness comes through loving and caring for them. Lord, we pray for the children, that they develop fully and completely. Help them to know your love, and may they in turn be able to live out this love and find peace and happiness. Amen.

- *What are some factors that cause conflict between parents and their children?*

- *What are some personal problems parents have to overcome before they can truly love?*

- *What can we do to help parents and children who are always in conflict?*

Parent-Teacher Interviews

I prayed, and understanding was given me; I called on God, and the spirit of wisdom came to me. **WISDOM 7:7**

Bless these conversations, Lord

Dear God, give us the discipline and strength to always do our best. We pray for the gift of appreciation and dedication. As our parents and teachers discuss our progress, may they remain open to our uniqueness, and may their discussions lead to our academic and spiritual growth. If we are not doing well in school, we pray that our parents and teachers can help us discover those areas we will excel in. We ask for a special blessing on all teachers and staff who work for our enrichment and development. May they be open to the Spirit and work toward a strong, vibrant, and Christlike community. Amen.

- *Are parent-teacher interviews useful?*

- *What should be some of the outcomes from a parent-teacher interview?*

- *Why do parents and teachers sometimes find it difficult to understand teens?*

Let it be a good day

Dear Lord, as our parents/guardians meet our teachers, we pray that this day goes well. We do not want our parents to be disappointed by our progress. We do not want our teachers to be upset if our parents feel we can do better. We ask you, Lord, for your blessing on this day and on the discussions that take place. We pray that we can all work together to assist us in achieving excellence, and that today will also lead to instilling in us a confidence and a work ethic that are pleasing to all. Amen.

- *Do parents and/or teachers have excessive expectations of us?*

- *What can teachers do to enable students to perform to the best of their ability?*

- *What changes can be made as a community to help students succeed in school?*

Patience

But as servants of God we have commended ourselves in every way: through great endurance, in afflictions, hardships, calamities, beatings, imprisonment, riots, labors, sleepless nights, hunger; by purity knowledge, patience, kindness, holiness of spirit, genuine love, truthful speech, and the power of God. **2 CORINTHIANS 6:4–7A**

Let's keep our cool

Patient and loving God, it is not always easy to remain patient. At times in our life we get angry, frustrated, and fed up. At these times we may say things we regret and do things that we wish we had not done. Help us to always maintain patience. May we always take a minute to think before we act or speak. If we are blessed with patience, this will help us to hold back and not do things that cannot be undone and not say things that cannot be taken back. For those times when we lost our patience, we ask for forgiveness from those whom we offended and hurt. May they know that when we act in moments of high emotion, it is not a reflection of our true thoughts. May mercy and forgiveness be ours, O Lord. Help us to move forward with more patience and understanding. Amen.

- *Does everyone lose their cool at some point in their lives?*

- *Why is patience such a difficult virtue to acquire?*

- *What strategies can we implement to acquire patience and stay calm?*

Things will work out

Dear Lord, we must learn to be patient and allow time to let things unfold as they should. Whether it be a test result, a phone call from a friend, admittance to college, or a call back from a job interview, help us to truly trust in you. Sometimes we do not get the results we want. If we have complete trust, then we will be able to accept whatever comes our way. Help us, Lord, to be surrendering and accepting, patient and trusting, so that no matter the outcome we will accept it and it may lead us down an even better path. Amen.

- *Can plans go terribly wrong in life but end up well?*

- *How can we learn to trust in God? How can we "let go and let God"?*

- *How can being patient with a parent or friend end up being a great blessing?*

Peace

"All who take the sword will perish by the sword." **MATTHEW 26:52**

Peace, not violence

Prince of Peace, today we pray for peace in our hearts, in our minds, and in our actions. In a world that is struggling to find meaning and often finds itself witnessing deliberate acts of violence, help us be peacemakers. Grant us the wisdom, insight, and prudence to be able to distinguish the need and necessity to resolve issues and conflicts without violence. Grant us the vision to recognize that although we are all unique and different, we share a commonality rooted in our humanity, dignity, and worth. Help us to embrace the model that you lived and to love one another as you continue to love us. Amen.

- *What can we do in our own community to promote peace?*

- *What creates a culture of violence? How can we counter these influences?*

- *Do we have to obtain inner peace before we can accomplish world peace?*

Let's resolve disputes through peace

Lord, we know that many things can be resolved through peaceful protest, negotiation, and dialogue. We look at the example of Mahatma Gandhi, who achieved greatness through a peaceful approach. He attained more through peace than others have attained through fighting wars. Lord, help us to be peacemakers. Help us to always attempt to reconcile through peaceful methods. May our efforts in turn bring peace to our communities and to the world. Amen.

- *Do those who take a peaceful approach have greater accomplishments? Example?*

- *Are there other great leaders who accomplished great things through peace?*

- *Are there times when peace will not work and we have to resort to aggression?*

Perseverance

Do you not know that in the race all the runners compete,
but only one receives the prize? Run in such a way that you may win it.
1 CORINTHIANS 9:24

Never give up

Lord, it is not easy to keep moving forward when we have attempted things and feel that we have failed. Whether it be rewriting a test, working on a friendship, attaining a personal best in sports, or passing a course, help us realize that it is not how many times we fall that is important. What is important is that we keep getting up. Help us to never give up and always give the best we have so that we may succeed in all we do. Amen.

- *What can we do to adopt a never-give-up attitude?*

- *Do we admire people who demonstrate great perseverance?*

- *Who are some great people who failed but never gave up and eventually experienced great success?*

Give it our all

Dear Lord, we know that when we work hard at things and finally achieve them, we appreciate them more. Help us to always be willing to give one hundred percent to all we do. Give us the fortitude to never give up but to continue through the hard times toward success. May we know that all things are possible through trust and faith in you. Grant us the confidence and strength we need to never give up and to find great satisfaction and fulfillment in our perseverance. Amen.

- *Can we find as much satisfaction in the effort as we do in the success?*

- *Why is it that many people give up if things don't work out the first time?*

- *What can help us to become people of perseverance and determination?*

Positive Attitude

Finally, beloved, whatever is true, whatever is honorable, whatever is just, whatever is pure, whatever is pleasing, whatever is commendable, if there is any excellence and if there is anything worthy of praise, think about these things. Keep on doing the things that you have learned and received and heard and seen in me, and the God of peace will be with you. **PHILIPPIANS 4:8–9**

Smile! It's free, and it's contagious

Dear God, at times, when we are facing sorrow, difficulty, and pain, it is difficult to smile. Today, we pray that we may see the good things in our lives. May we see the good, even in the pain and suffering. With this attitude we will be uplifted and inspired. It brings a smile to our face, makes our path easier to walk, and brings meaning to every part of our life. Keep us smiling and joyful. Amen.

- *How can we see the positive throughout the difficult times?*

- *Does our positive attitude impact on our happiness and the happiness of others?*

- *How do our loved ones feel when they see us smiling, even when we feel like crying?*

What difference does attitude make?

Dear Lord, we often hear of the importance of remaining positive. When we look at things with a positive attitude, things seem to go our way. However, it is not easy to stay positive. Help us to see things with joyful hearts and peaceful minds. May optimism fill our days, and peace fill our nights. Amen.

- *Who are people in history or in our lives who remain positive, no matter the situation?*

- *If we approach something with a positive attitude, does it affect the result?*

- *How can a negative attitude affect the outcome of a plan or career or goal?*

Prayerfulness

To you O Lord I lift up my soul, O My God, in you I trust. **PSALM 25:1-2**

Jesus is waiting to hear from you

Dear Jesus, we know how much you love to hear from us. May
we always take time to talk to you. May we be blessed with the
knowledge of your presence and your longing to hear our prayers.
We often find it difficult to take the time we should to talk to
you. We sometimes lack the patience or discipline, even though
we know that talking to you helps us enrich our lives. It clears
our minds, allows us to put things in perspective, and gives us the
opportunity to hear you direct us. Amen.

- *Where do you feel is the best place to pray? Where do you feel
  closest to Jesus?*

- *Does praying help us in other areas of our lives?*

- *Do you prefer saying traditional prayers or creating
  your own prayer? Why?*

Let's talk to God

Dear Lord, may we come to know and appreciate the power of
prayer. When we wake in the morning, you are there waiting for
a good morning greeting. When we are in a time of need, you are
there waiting to hear from us. When we go through the day, you
are there waiting for a simple recognition and smile from us.
When we go to bed at night, you are there waiting to hear about
our day. Lord, help us to be a more prayerful people. We know
that the more we talk to you, the better we get to know you. Great
things will happen in getting to know you better. Help us not to be

strangers to you, O Lord; rather, help us to be your friends, talking to you and praying to you daily. Amen.

- *Is talking to God like talking to a friend? Is it as useful?*

- *Does prayer make us more clear-minded and stronger?*

- *What kinds of things may we feel comfortable only talking to God about?*

Pressure

I pray that, according to the riches of his glory, he may grant that you may be strengthened in your inner being with power through his Spirit and that Christ may dwell in your hearts through faith as you are being rooted and grounded in love. **EPHESIANS 3:16–17**

Too much pressure

Dear Lord, life is filled with pressure. There is pressure to get our work done, to get a part-time job, and to get good grades. There is pressure to do things that we do not want to do. We pray that when we are overwhelmed with pressure we will feel your peace. We pray that we will see that all things pass and that with you at our side we can go through any difficulty. We trust, Lord, that you are there to bring us comfort and assurance during times of great pressure. Amen.

- *What are some of the areas in life where we experience pressure?*

- *What can we do to help take the pressure off?*

- *Is pressure ever a good thing? At what point does pressure become harmful?*

Peer pressure is tough

Dear Lord, we are all faced with peer pressure. It often causes us to do things we are not comfortable with, and it gets us into trouble. Help us to be able to stand up to peer pressure. Whenever we are contemplating doing something that does not represent who we truly are, grant us the ability to pause, reflect, and choose otherwise. Lord, may we have the strength and self-confidence to always remain true to ourselves. Help us to recognize that true friends will never pressure us but rather encourage us to be the best person we can be. Amen.

- *Do people ever do things that they don't want to do because of peer pressure?*

- *What happens when people stand up to the peer pressure?*

- *Do true friends pressure others to do things that they don't want to or are harmful?*

Progress Reports

For it is God who is at work in you, enabling you both to will and to work for his good pleasure. **PHILIPPIANS 2:13**

Keep us progressing

Dear Lord, today we receive our progress reports. We pray that none of us is shocked by our grades or the comments that teachers have made about us. We pray that our families and our teachers will understand us and that their comments will reflect this understanding. May each of us be willing to work to our full potential, and may our parents and teachers find this effort to be admirable. And we pray, Lord, that we remain confident in ourselves, filled with the positive self-esteem you have created us with. Amen.

- *Is trying our hardest good enough, even when we perform poorly?*

- *Are progress reports helpful? Why or why not?*

- *What should we do when we feel marks or comments are unfair?*

Keep us confident

Dear Lord, we pray that these reports today will lead us to understand the areas in which we are strong and the areas in which we need improvement. Grant us the confidence to be able to discuss with our teachers our grades as well as the comments that they have made. If we believe that these comments do not truly reflect our efforts and ability, help us to respectfully say this to our teachers. May today be a new beginning where we are able to improve upon our work, and all those involved in our education are able to gain a better understanding of who we are and what are our true abilities. Amen.

- *Do students feel comfortable discussing their marks and progress with their teachers?*

- *Are some teachers easier to discuss this with than others?*

- *What are the keys to a successful discussion?*

Purposefulness

I am grateful to Christ Jesus our Lord, who has strengthened me, because he judged me faithful and appointed me to his service. **1 TIMOTHY 1:12**

Help me find my way

Lord, sometimes I have no idea what I am to do. I do not know what courses to take, what career to aim for, what friends to hang with, what clothes to buy, and what phone to purchase. Help me, Lord, in all my decisions. May they be rooted in fulfilling some greater purpose. Help me to get beyond the moment and see the greater purpose to my life. Grant me the wisdom and insight I need to make decisions that are meaningful and that will result in a life of joy and peace. Amen.

- *What resources can someone use to help make good decisions?*

- *Do people tend to look at immediate results rather than the larger purpose of their lives?*

- *Do we have people to help us with discovering our purpose in life?*

Everyone has a purpose

Dear Lord, help us to recognize that everyone in this world has a purpose. It does not matter what we look like or what ability we possess. It does not matter how strong or weak we are. It does not matter how well or poorly we do in school. We all have a purpose. We know that each of us is a child of God and every child of God has a purpose. Help us, Lord, to treat each other respectfully and with kindness, helping each other find our special role in life. Amen.

- *Does everyone have a purpose?*

- *Does purpose require physical or intellectual ability? Discuss.*

- *Why do some people find it so difficult to discover their purpose in life?*

Purpose (To Find)

Now to him who by the power at work within us is able to accomplish abundantly far more than all we can ask or imagine, to him be glory in the church and in Christ Jesus to all generations, forever and ever. Amen.

EPHESIANS 3:20–21

Trust in God's plan

Lord, as Cardinal Newman said in a meditation: "God has created me to do him some definite service; he has committed some work to me which he has not committed to another. I have my mission—I may never know it in this life, but I shall be told it in the next. I am a link in the chain. A bond of connection between persons." Grant us the spiritual grace we need to follow your way. Grant us the strength we need to abandon our own goals and to replace them with your goals for us. Grant us the love we need to be able to attain our purpose with a joyful and cheerful heart. Grant us the ability to work together to accomplish our mission. We ask this through you, O Lord, our friend and our Savior. Amen.

- *Is Cardinal Newman right when he said God has a purpose for each of us?*

- *How do we come to know our purpose? Who can help us in this search?*

■ *How does it leave a person feeling if they cannot find their purpose?*

Reveal our purpose

Dear Lord, we know that each of us has a purpose. Help us to come to know our true selves so that our purpose may be revealed more clearly to us. At times we go through periods of darkness, not knowing the purpose to our lives. Let us not be discouraged, Lord. Help us to see the light. Help us to see the divine within us and to live this nature out. Help us to be dedicated to knowing and fulfilling our purpose. Amen.

■ *How do we better understand who we are and what our mission in life is?*

■ *Do people often deviate from what they are meant to do/be? Why?*

■ *Are we still too young to know our purpose in life? If so, at what age should we know?*

Rejection

After a little while the bystander came up and said to Peter, "certainly you are also one of them, for your accent betrays you." Then he began to curse, and he swore an oath, "I do not know the man!" At that moment the cock crowed. **MATTHEW 26:73-74**

Soldier on

All-accepting God, it is painful to be rejected. It can bring on despair, anger, and suffering. We pray for the strength to endure it. Help us to never measure ourselves and our worth through rejection. Keep us confident in who we are and aware of the talents and gifts we possess. When we have one door slammed in our face, we pray for the perseverance to knock on another door. May we never let one person's rejection affect the greatness that we have within us. Amen.

- *How does it affect people when they experience rejection?*

- *Why do people allow rejection to affect them so much?*

- *Can a person be rejected in one community and be accepted in another?*

Everyone experiences rejection

Dear Lord, there will be times in our lives where we experience rejection. When we do experience this, help us to not lose confidence in ourselves. Help us to understand that rejection is a part of life. It does not mean we are not capable, not worthy, or not a good person. Help us to always put rejection in perspective, and may it never prevent us from moving forward. We pray that rejection does not discourage us from believing in ourselves. With belief in ourselves and in you, we will be inspired to move forward. Amen.

- *Can rejection ever be healthy or beneficial?*

- *Why are some people more motivated to succeed after being rejected?*

- *Many great people in history experienced many rejections. How did it motivate them?*

Relationship (Boyfriend/Girlfriend)

Therefore, be imitators of God, as beloved children, and live in love, as Christ loved us and gave himself up for us, a fragrant offering and sacrifice to God. **EPHESIANS 5:1–2**

Another relationship over

Lord, it is difficult to experience and endure the end of a relationship. We pray today for all those who are suffering the loneliness of failing relationships. Help them to know that there is a person or calling for them. May their suffering of the loss of their relationship be eased. Help them to realize that although these times are difficult, they also offer potential to grow. We offer up our sadness to you, O Lord, and may all be comforted and consoled. Amen.

- *What is the purpose of dating for a long period of time?*

- *Why do some relationships work out and others do not?*

- *How can a relationship that has failed make us better people?*

Love is great

Dear Lord, relationships are a big part of our lives. As we enter into or continue with our dating, help us to choose people who make us shine. May our relationships always bring out the best in us. May we be respected for who we are and not be asked to become someone we are not. Lord, bless our relationships with love, always making us better people. Amen.

- *In what ways do we become a better person if we are in a healthy relationship?*

- *In what ways can a boyfriend or girlfriend bring out the worst in us? Explain.*

- *Should we warn a friend whom we think is in a bad relationship?*

Reliability

[Jesus put before the people] another parable: "The kingdom of heaven is like a mustard seed that someone took and sowed in his field; it is the smallest of all the seeds, but when it has grown it is the greatest of shrubs and becomes a tree, so that the birds of the air come and make nests in its branches." MATTHEW 13:31–32

You can rely on me

Dear Lord, one of the greatest needs that our friends have is the ability to be able to rely on us. We pray that we will have the courage, discipline, and strength to always be there for our friends. Help us to recognize the importance of keeping our word. Help us to appreciate the confidence that others have in us. We pray that, as difficult as it may sometimes be, we will be reliable— now and always. Amen.

- *How important is it to be reliable to our family and friends?*

- *Are there times when we must break promises? If so, when and why?*

- *What are things that get in the way of us remaining reliable?*

Giving it our best

Dear Lord, we always want others to be able to rely on us. However, sometimes the responsibility is grave and almost impossible to carry out. Help us during these times to never become overwhelmed; rather, help us to take things in stride and know that if we are doing our best, that is all we can do. You do not expect more from us than we are capable of giving. Help us and others to realize and to respect this. We ask this through you, O Lord. Amen.

- *When we get overwhelmed, what helps us to slow down and put things in perspective?*

- *What do we do if we make a promise and then realize it was not a good promise to make?*

- *Can we be viewed as reliable if we try our best but do not succeed?*

Report Cards

So let us not grow weary in doing what is right, for we will reap at harvest time, if we do not give up. **GALATIANS 6:9**

Looking for the personal best

Dear God, today will be a good day for some and not so good for others. As we receive our report cards, we ask that you watch over each of us. Some of us will be happy with the results, and some of us will not. Help us to accept our grades and always be satisfied with what we have received because we have done our best. If we have neglected our studies, we pray for more self-discipline so that we will work to our full potential. Help our parents/ guardians to understand our capabilities and to support us always as we work to attain our personal best. Amen.

- *Can anyone ever ask you for more than your best?*

- *How do we know when we have given it our best?*

- *What do we need to do to ensure that we are able to do our best?*

Hope the family is satisfied

Dear Lord, today we receive our report cards. Even though we have tried our best, we know that our family may be disappointed in our grades. Lord, help our families to understand that we are working to the best of our ability. Help them to accept that our best is all we can give. Give to them the insight to see that we have great potential and that our abilities may lie in areas that are not reflected by our grades. Help them see the light, O Lord; for this, we will be forever grateful. Amen.

- *Why do family members want more even when they see us working hard?*

- *How does it make a teen feel when their family is not satisfied with their results?*

- *How does it make us feel when we know we are not working to our potential?*

Respect

Have fellowship with the Spirit and...have kindness and compassion for one another. **PHILIPPIANS 2:1B (GOOD NEWS TRANSLATION)**

Dignity of each person

Ever-present God, we pray that each of us be granted the spiritual blessing to come to a full awareness of what it means to be made in your image. Each and every one of us has been made in your image, in your love, wisdom, and beauty. May this in turn provide us with the confidence and courage we need to give respect and dignity to every person. May all that we say and do show respect for others and bring your love to them. Amen.

- *Should every person in the world be granted respect or do they have to earn it?*

- *Can people lose our respect? If they do, can they gain it back?*

- *As a school community, how can we promote an attitude of respect for every person?*

I want respect

Dear God, you have taught us that just by being human we deserve respect. Yet we do not always get the respect we desire. We have done nothing wrong, and people still do not respect us. Help them to see us as their brothers and sisters, to witness our strengths and see the valuable gifts that we can offer to this community. May they see that their inability to give respect not only hurts us, but it also hurts them, denying them all that we have to offer. Amen.

- *Why do people find it difficult to show respect to others?*

- *When people prejudge others negatively, does it create a poor school community?*

- *How do we react when we see peers not respecting their teachers, parents, or friends?*

Responsibilities

For he has graciously granted you the privilege not only of believing in Christ, but of suffering for him as well. **PHILIPPIANS 1:29**

God, help me through this

Lord, as teenagers we are given a great deal of responsibility. We have high expectations placed on us, and we are young at heart. Help us to fulfill our responsibilities that are reasonable, and help others to recognize responsibilities that are unreasonable. May we never be overwhelmed, and may we always be willing to respectfully challenge others when the responsibilities are unreasonable or more than we can handle. Amen.

- *Does society understand what it is like to be a teenager? Explain.*

- *Does society expect too much from or not enough from young people?*

- *To whom can we turn to for help when we are dealing with more than we can handle?*

Responsibilities help us grow

Dear God, help us to recognize that responsibilities are an opportunity for growth and development. They are placed upon us by parents, teachers, and a society that wants us to excel. May we be blessed with responsibilities that enable us to recognize and develop the gifts with which we have been blessed. May they present challenges that force us to be the best we can be. Amen.

- *In what ways can responsibilities be positive?*

- *When has an opportunity that you were given helped you discover or develop your gifts?*

- *What leaders have been given responsibilities that forced them to excel?*

Sacrifice

"Those who find their life will lose it, and those who lose their life for my sake will find it." **MATTHEW 10:39**

Give it up

Dear Lord, as difficult as it is, we pray that we will have the discipline and willingness to make sacrifices. Help us to recognize that it is in and through sacrifice that we will accomplish great things. When we are willing to give up something for a cause that is greater than we are, it can only bring us success and a great feeling of accomplishment. Lord, help us to be people who are always willing to sacrifice for the benefit of greater causes. Amen.

- *Should making sacrifices be a part of our everyday life?*

- *In what ways do people who make sacrifices benefit?*

- *Who are some people who have sacrificed for you? How did it make you a better person?*

Sacrifice is worth it

Lord, we know that sacrifice is a part of life. If we want to do well on tests, we must sacrifice our social time to study. If we want to do well on the court, field, or stage, we have to sacrifice our time to practice. If we want to do well in life, we have to sacrifice immediate pleasure for long-term gain. Grant us the wisdom to know what we need to sacrifice and the strength to make the sacrifice, so that we can be the best we can be.

Amen.

- *Who are some people in history who made great sacrifices to create a better world?*

- *What are some sacrifices that we can make that will pay off in the end?*

- *How did the sacrifices Jesus made change the world?*

School Spirit

Make my joy complete: be of the same mind, having the same love, being in full accord and of one mind. Do nothing from selfish ambition or conceit, but in humility regard others as better than yourselves. Let each of you look not to your own interests, but to the interests of others. **PHILIPPIANS 2:2-4**

Making each other great

Lord, you call us to live the Golden Rule: to treat others as we would like to be treated. We pray that we will live out your calling, treating each person in our school just as we would like to be treated. We are one family, living as brothers and sisters, working together to elevate each other, to enhance each other's gifts, and to build your kingdom. With your guidance and love, we strive to build a strong community here at (*name of school*), along with a bright future for our school and each other.

- *The church has many groups. In what ways can we offer our gifts in its mission?*

- *In what ways can we enhance the hidden gifts of others?*

- *In what ways can our school better foster a spiritually based community?*

Let's keep the spirit alive

Lord, we have an amazing school community. Help us to do all we can to contribute to creating the best possible atmosphere here at (*name of school*). Help us to recognize that the way to do this is through challenging one another to get involved in school activities and to love and respect one another. We strive, Lord, to live out your message in all that we do and all that we say. Amen.

- *How can we encourage students and staff to participate in school activities?*

- *What can we do to ensure that all students and staff are respected?*

- *How does a strong school spirit lead to greater success?*

School Work

For this very reason, you must make every effort to support your faith with goodness, and goodness with knowledge, and knowledge with self-control, and self-control with endurance, and endurance with godliness, and godliness with mutual affection, and mutual affection with love. **2 PETER 1:5-7**

Homework....Yuck!

Lord, we do not like doing homework. It involves staying up late, sacrificing social time, and putting in a great deal of concentration and effort. Yet we know that this work helps us excel in the long run. Today, we pray that we will be able to continue to keep up with our school work. We pray that we will find the proper balance in life and be able to give the time and attention to the work that is required. Lord, grant us the discipline, strength, and perseverance we need to succeed in our school work. Amen.

- *In what ways can we make doing homework more fun?*

- *How do we balance school work with social time, sports, and other responsibilities?*

- *Why is it important to do our homework? How does it benefit us in the long run?*

Hard work may help us

Dear Lord, we do not like it when we feel that we are being overwhelmed with demands. Often we do not feel like we can even complete our homework. We struggle with this, and it puts a great deal of pressure upon us. Help us to take each day as it comes. Give us the gift of patience and help us to remain calm. We know that if we approach every situation with the knowledge that you are with us, we are sure to be calm and at peace. Amen.

- *Will hard work make us feel good about ourselves and make us better people?*

- *Do people who work harder tend to succeed more?*

- *How does working hard in school represent what we will face in the workforce?*

Self (View Of)

The Lord created human beings out of earth...He endowed them with strength like his own and made them in his own image. **SIRACH 17:1, 3**

We are great

Dear Lord, we are all created equal; however, we look and feel very different. Some have great looks and wonderful personalities. Others have great love, compassion, and understanding. Others have great intelligence and problem-solving abilities. Help us, no matter what our strengths, to recognize the value in ourselves. We often look at the gifts of others as greater than our own. Help us to see that our gifts are equally valuable and that, as your children, we are all created with infinite value. Amen.

- *How do we maintain a positive view and see the value of our own gifts?*

- *Do we generally value the gifts of others as more important than our own?*

- *What does it mean when we say that "the grass is always greener on the other side"?*

I am beautiful

Dear Lord, when we look at magazine ads, television commercials, and billboards, we see many images of men and women that do not look like us. The media create an idea of beauty that is hard to achieve. Help us to recognize that we have infinite beauty merely by being one of your children. Help us to see the shallowness in society's view of what is important and beautiful. Lord, grant us the gift of discernment so that we are able to know the difference between what is true and what is false. Amen.

- *What does society define as beautiful? Do you agree or disagree?*

- *What is the impact of media and advertising on our concept of beauty and self-worth?*

- *Where do we look to find the truth about what is of value and beautiful?*

Self Discipline

You shall love the Lord your God with all your heart, and with all your soul, and with all your mind, and with all your strength. **MARK 12:30–31**

No pain, no gain

Dear God, discipline is an extremely important gift. It is in and through discipline that we are able to do well in school. Discipline results in us doing the work to keep our minds and bodies fit. It is through discipline that we can overcome any obstacle and live a more ordered life, filled with successes. God, grant us discipline in order that we may live out our gifts fully and develop to the best of our potential. Amen.

- *How can the gift of self-discipline make us more successful and fulfilled persons?*

- *How can we develop the gift of self-discipline?*

- *Does society encourage and challenge us to live a disciplined life?*

Discipline produces great results

Dear Jesus, you are a wonderful example to us of a person with great self-discipline. You continuously sacrificed yourself in order to create a better world and attain your Father's will. We know that when we possess self-discipline, we will be capable of achieving great things. Jesus, grant us the self-discipline to be able to sacrifice that which needs to be sacrificed in order for us to attain a greater good. May we be blessed with the ability to deny ourselves so that in the end we may attain greatness. Amen.

- *What are some of the sacrifices Jesus made to accomplish his mission?*

- *Who are some people who taught us that self-discipline pays off?*

- *How do great athletes, missionaries, and others acquire the gift of self-discipline?*

Service

"Whoever wishes to be great among you must be your servant, and whoever wishes to be first among you must be your slave." **MATTHEW 20:26B–27**

Created for one another

Jesus, Prince of Peace, you said, "Come, follow me." In our decision to follow you, help us to model your love, mercy, and forgiveness. Grant us the ability to embrace the outcast, protect the weak, give to the poor, and forgive those who hurt us. In these ways we will truly be a person for others. We will play an important part in healing a broken world and building your kingdom. Amen.

- *What does it mean to live in a world as brothers and sisters?*

- *How much time in our day should we be dedicating to serving others?*

- *In what ways is our school community a servant to the world?*

Everyone needs comfort

Dear God, help us to create an environment where every student has someone to turn to when they are in need. May each student have a place to go when they are alone and need comfort, a person to turn to when they are lost or frightened, a shoulder to lean on when they are sad and discouraged, and people who believe in them when they feel defeated. God, give us the gifts to better know and understand others and be a person for others. Amen.

- *In what ways are we there to help those in our school who are in need?*

- *How do we know when someone is struggling? What signs does this person show?*

- *Are we admired or criticized by peers when we are always there for others?*

Siblings

Let us therefore no longer pass judgment on one another, but resolve instead never to put a stumbling block or hindrance in the way of another.
ROMANS 14:13

I want to be a good sibling

Dear God, our siblings rely on us. Our relationships are not short-term. Our brother or sister is our family forever. There is a special bond that cannot be found in other relationships. They sometimes look to us for advice, for support, or simply for understanding. For some we are their hero, their lifeline in their struggles. We pray

that we are always a good brother/sister to them, offering them all
that they need to be the very best they can be. Amen.

- *In what ways is a brother or sister a special relationship,*
  unlike any other?

- *What are some things our siblings rely on us for? How can we be*
  a better brother/sister?

- *What are some activities we can do with our siblings to build*
  stronger relationships?

Forgiving is a part of family living

Dear Lord, we sometimes fight in our family. We fight over simple
things like who chooses the channel, who gets the car, or who does
household chores. It is normal to have some disagreements, but
we pray that we will always show the love we have for our siblings.
We will make the sacrifices to bring them greater comfort. May
we always show our appreciation and let them know that this is a
valued lifelong relationship. Amen.

- *Why do some families fight a lot and others hardly at all?*

- *Do people regret it when they mistreat or neglect their sibling?*

- *How does it make us feel when we see grown-ups close*
  to their siblings?

Special Intentions

"So I say to you, Ask, and it will be given you; search and you will find; knock and the door will be opened for you. For everyone who asks receives, and everyone who searches finds, and for everyone who knocks, the door will be opened." **LUKE 11:9–10**

Lord, hear our prayer

Saving God, today we pray for all the intentions that we hold in our hearts. (*pause/prayer requests*) We lift these prayer requests to you and ask for your mercy and goodness. Help us to recognize your presence among us and to find comfort and peace in your love and concern for us. Help us to know that no request goes unheard and to trust in your goodness, kindness, and compassion. Amen.

- *We know that God hears all our prayers. If this is the case, why are they not all granted?*

- *What does it mean to trust in God's way?*

- *Do we sometimes pray for something that we later realized was not good for us?*

Ask and you shall receive

Dear Lord, we know that you tell us to ask and we shall receive; however, sometimes we ask and our requests are not granted. Help us to be a prayerful people who ultimately trust in you. We often feel that we know what is best for ourselves and our friends. May our faith keep us humble, help us realize the limitations we have, and let us see that it is your way we need to come to accept. Amen.

- *What did Jesus mean when he said, "Ask and you shall receive"?*

- *Who are some people who did not receive what they prayed for?*

- *If a prayer request is not granted should we stop praying for things? Discuss.*

Special Person

Now therefore, if you obey my voice and keep my covenant, you shall be my treasured possession out of all peoples. **EXODUS 19:5**

Special people make all the difference

Dear God, we want to give thanks today for that special person we hold in our hearts. We offer this prayer for them. They have done so much for us that we cannot even begin to express how they have impacted our lives. We pray that they be rewarded for their goodness, that their lives be filled with joy and peace, and that all they do for others may one day be returned unto them. Amen.

- *Is it important to pray for people we love? What difference does it make?*

- *Do you think that good people are generally rewarded for their goodness?*

- *How do we show people that we are grateful for all they do for us?*

Lord, accept my prayer for my friend

Dear Lord, we come to you today, asking for a special blessing on one of our friends. We know that they are in need of our prayers, and we ask that you show your mercy and love to them. Be with them as they venture through this difficult time. May they be comforted in the knowledge that they are loved, and strengthened in the knowledge that they do not walk alone. Amen.

- *People often go through difficult times. When they do, how can we help them?*

- *How do we know when we are "crossing the line" when we reach out to help a friend?*

- *Do we underestimate how much we can help to save a friend from something terrible?*

Strength

Jesus answered them, "The hour has come for the Son of Man to be glorified." **JOHN 12:23**

I need strength

God of strength, as we work through this semester, we need to find strength. We are faced with so many different challenges, and we are being pulled in so many different directions. Help us to find the strength we need to persevere and to perform to the best of our ability. May we acquire the virtue of humility, never hesitating to find our strength through you, friends, family, or teachers. We ask this through Christ our Lord. Amen.

- *Where do we find strength? What did Jesus do when he needed strength?*

- *Why are we sometimes ashamed to ask others for help?*

■ *Do we view strength as something we only have when we are able to "walk alone"?*

Keep us strong

God of strength, we all have times in our lives when we feel that we are going to break down. This may happen at the most unusual times and over very silly things. However, we all recognize that these times result from a buildup of numerous events and incidents that we have going on in our lives. We pray today for the strength to keep our composure. Help us to recognize that this difficult time is only temporary and will pass. Help us to see that there is light at the end of every tunnel, and that all we need is the strength to endure these difficult times. Amen.

■ *Does everyone have moments of weakness in their lives?*

■ *Do we tend to view depression and unhappiness as lifelong or temporary?*

■ *What can we do to overcome a few months or even a few years of difficult times?*

Student Council (New)

Jesus said, "Let the little children come to me, and do not stop them; for it is to such as these that the kingdom of heaven belongs." MATTHEW 19:14

Let the planning begin

Dear Lord, as our new student council is proclaimed, we pray for them and for their efforts in this upcoming year. May each of us do all we can to support and encourage them as they work to provide us with a fun and memorable year. Grant us the willingness to sacrifice for them and for this community in order to make this upcoming year the best one yet. We ask this through Jesus our Lord and Savior. Amen.

- *What makes a student council successful?*

- *Do the contributions of the student body matter? Why or why not?*

- *What makes a school year memorable?*

Thanks in advance

Dear Lord, today we pray for our student council. We know that the positions on council require a lot of hard work and a big time commitment. We ask you to watch over our council. Bless this council with the ability to work as a team with the best interests of all the students in their plans. We pray they will succeed at doing all the things they wish to accomplish this year. Amen.

- *What are the challenges of student council members?*

- *How can we as a community make their job easier?*

- *How is being on student council being a servant as much as it is being a leader?*

Student Council Elections

Here is my servant, whom I uphold, my chosen, in whom my soul delights.
ISAIAH 42:1

May the best person win!

Dear Lord, as we prepare to vote for our student council, we pray that each person will give thought to this important decision. We hope to elect a council that will lead us into a great year here at (*name of school*). We pray that we can get beyond popularity to truth. We pray that we can overcome peer pressure and attain authenticity. Help us to be wise and prudent as we make our decisions and cast our votes. Amen.

- *What causes people to vote for certain people? Is popularity sometimes the motive?*

- *Does the best person always win?*

- *How can we help to ensure that the best candidate is chosen?*

It takes guts to run

God of courage, we pray for all those who have stepped forward to run for student council. We know that this is not an easy decision. It takes courage and dedication to run for a position. May the students of our school appreciate the dedication of the candidates and offer all of them our thanks and appreciation. May they know that we are proud of them and their willingness to put their names forward to run for election. We ask this through Christ our Lord. Amen.

- *How can we encourage people whom we know would be great, to run for council?*

- *Does the thought of failure prevent some from running for student council?*

- *What does it mean to succeed? Can someone lose and still have succeeded?*

Suffering

From that time on, Jesus began to show his disciples that he must go to Jerusalem and undergo great suffering at the hands of the elders and chief priests and scribes, and be killed, and on the third day be raised.

MATTHEW 16:21

Embracing our own crosses

Dear Jesus, when life presents us with difficulties and pain, help us to look to your own suffering and be strengthened. Your passion, death, and resurrection help us to embrace our own suffering. When we confront obstacles that cause us to suffer, we feel your presence and begin anew. When we are the victims of injustice, you carry our cross with us. Jesus, continue to give us strength, comfort, and consolation. With you we can overcome all suffering. Amen.

- *What are some of the things that can help us in times of suffering?*

- *Why do some people have to suffer more than others?*

- *In what ways is Jesus with us when we go through suffering?*

Lord, we need healing

Healing God, we witness suffering every day. We pray today that you will extend your healing touch to our loved ones. Help us to recognize that even in our darkest moments you are always there for us, as you were when your own Son suffered. Grant us the wisdom and compassion to serve as your instruments here on earth as we walk beside those who are suffering. May we be a source of light in their darkest times and a source of strength in their weakest times. We ask this through Jesus, who made the greatest sacrifice in love and service to us. Amen.

- *In what ways can we reach out and help those who are suffering?*

- *What are some of the things we can learn from our own suffering and that of others?*

- *Is greatness forged out of suffering?*

Teachers/Support Staff

And we sent Timothy, our brother and co-worker for God in proclaiming the gospel of Christ, to strengthen and encourage you for the sake of your faith. **1 THESSALONIANS 3:2**

Praying for our staff

Dear God, please provide each of the staff in this school with a sense of peace. As they continue to contribute to making our education possible, grant them the awareness of our appreciation for all they do. We know that we would not be able to grow in knowledge and faith if it were not for their efforts. Bless them for all their good work. Be with them, Lord, and help them to feel your presence, support, and love. Amen.

- *How can we better express our appreciation to our teachers and support staff?*

- *What are some of the things that we appreciate most about them?*

- *In what ways are we all called to be teachers?*

Special teachers change our lives

Dear Lord, today we give you thanks for our teachers. We wish
to make special mention of those teachers who spend extra time
to help us understand, who are interested in how we are doing,
who are willing to go out of their way when we are in need, and
who truly care about us. We know, Lord, that in years to come,
we may not remember the lesson these teachers taught us in
class; however, we will remember the lessons they taught us
in life. They have instilled in us through their own actions and
words the importance of love, respect, and caring for one another.
Lord, bless these teachers for all they do, and may they know the
appreciation we hold in our hearts for them. Amen.

- *What makes the profession of teaching very special?*

- *Who are some important teachers in our lives outside of school?*

- *Who are some leaders in our community who have also taught us
  great things?*

Temptation

Blessed is anyone who endures temptation. Such a one has stood the test
and will receive the crown of life that the Lord has promised to those who
love him. JAMES 1:12

We strive for greatness

All powerful and loving God, we are faced with many rules and
laws and are constantly provided with temptations to break
those rules and laws. Many temptations are difficult to resist
because they offer excitement and acceptance into a group. We

pray to you, God, asking for the knowledge to comprehend the destruction they bring, the prudence to discern good from bad, and the self-discipline to resist these temptations. With your grace, God, we can resist temptations that will destroy us, and we can focus on those things that will build us up and make us great people. Loving God, we strive for greatness. Amen.

- *What are some of the greatest temptations that we face each day?*

- *Do people tend to look at the short-term or long-term consequences of their actions?*

- *Where can we find the strength or resolve to avoid temptation?*

You are there when we fall

Dear God, sometimes we can recognize that which is destructive, but we find it difficult to avoid temptation. Our hearts and minds tell us the path to choose, but we sometimes take the easier route. As a result, we may have many destructive experiences and fall to our knees. We ask you, God, to be there for us in all that we do. We need you to guide us to make the right choices and to be there when we make the wrong choices. Your ever-present mercy and support will lift us up so that we can continue on a righteous path and bring healing and greatness to our community and world. Amen.

- *Why is it sometimes difficult to forgive ourselves when we make mistakes?*

- *In what ways do temptations that are evil present themselves as good?*

- *Do you agree that God's mercy is infinite? What does this mean?*

Tests/Assignments

The fruit of the Spirit is love, joy, peace, patience, kindness, goodness, faithfulness, gentleness and self-control. **GALATIANS 5:22–23**

A+

Dear Lord, we have studied a great deal for this test. We pray that our performance on this test truly reflects the hard work we did preparing. We pray that we will maintain a sense of calm so that we may attain our personal best. Help us, Lord, to do well on the test. Amen.

- *What are some strategies that are effective in understanding and retaining information?*

- *Are tests an accurate measure of how well a person knows the material?*

- *Do anxiety and worry affect one's performance in a good way or bad way?*

Balancing a busy schedule is tough

Dear Lord, life is very busy. We are pulled in many different directions. Some of us have jobs; others are on teams; others are caring for someone who is ill at home; and some of us struggle with our own illness. Lord, help us, no matter what our obstacle, to do well on this test/assignment. Be with us as we strive to succeed. May the knowledge of your presence help to reassure us of our ability and enable us to do well. We ask this through Christ our Lord. Amen.

- *What are strategies we can use to do all that is expected of us and still do well in school?*

- *How can we deal with things when there is simply too much stress?*

- *Will praying make us feel better and perform better?*

Thankfulness

Blessed be the God and Father of our Lord Jesus Christ, the Father of mercies and the God of all consolation. **2 CORINTHIANS 1:3**

Focus on the stars

God of blessings, today we give thanks for the blessings in our lives. We thank you for the gifts of the Holy Spirit, the positive attitude in the face of negativity, the light you offer in our darkness, the endless opportunities to fulfill our dreams, and the love we have because of your love for us. Thank you, God, for all these wonderful blessings. Amen.

- *In what ways does an attitude of thankfulness make our lives feel whole and rich?*

- *Do we tend to get so wrapped up in negativity that we forget to be thankful?*

- *Is it considered cool to be known as a person who is always thankful?*

Thank you, God, for great friends

God of friendships, today we give you thanks for all you have given us. We particularly give thanks for our friends. Friends are there to celebrate with us, to cry with us, to comfort us, and to support us. Life has far greater meaning when we are able to share it with friends. We thank you for our friends who serve as a glimpse of light in times of darkness, and hope in times of despair. Thank you, Lord, for the gift of our friends. Amen.

- *What are the qualities of a healthy friendship, and what does healthy friendship offer us?*

- *Does an attitude of thankfulness make our relationships with others stronger?*

- *Are we embarrassed to tell family, friends, and others, "I love you"?*

Tolerance

Bear with one another and, if anyone has a complaint against another, forgive each other; just as the Lord has forgiven you, so you also must forgive. **COLOSSIANS 3:13**

Let me not be bothered

Dear Lord, tolerance is a gift. When someone is annoying us, we pray for tolerance. When someone causes us trouble, we pray for tolerance. When someone is upsetting us, we pray for tolerance. When someone is gossiping about us, we pray for tolerance. Lord, grant us tolerance so that we may be understanding, respectful, and kind. Help us see that our good nature will have a powerful impact on others. Amen.

- *How does the virtue of tolerance benefit us in life?*

- *Are there times when we should not be tolerant? If so, when?*

- *What is it that allows some people to be more tolerant than others?*

Group work can be tough

Lord, getting along in groups is not always easy. Sometimes people find it hard to get along. They allow their egos to take control, and they always want to be in charge. They want to tell everyone what they should do and how to do it. In these situations we pray for tolerance. Help us to work gently, with a spirit of tolerance, with these people. In all that we do and with all the people with whom we interact, we pray for this spirit of tolerance so that we can all move in a more productive direction. Amen.

- *What are some strategies we can use to ensure that all members of a group get along?*

- *Can a spirit of tolerance help us realize that we may be wrong and in need of growth?*

- *What are some life lessons we can learn through working in a group?*

Trust

Jesus said to him, "If you wish to be perfect, go, sell your possessions, and give the money to the poor, and you will have treasure in heaven; then come, follow me." **MATTHEW 19:21**

The gift of trust

Trusting God, help us to be people who trust in you. Help us to trust others as well. We pray for wisdom and prudence so that we will not be taken advantage of, but we also pray for trust in others so that together great things can be accomplished. We pray to have trust in others so that they will believe in themselves. You love us, and we know that you trust us. We pray for that kind of trust with those we love. Amen.

- *Should we always trust? Are there times when it is better not to trust?*

- *How does the ability to trust make our lives richer?*

- *In what ways can a lack of trust destroy relationships?*

Grant us good judgment

Dear Lord, help us to know when we are able to trust others. We often are put in situations that demand our trust. May we be guided by the Holy Spirit in recognizing situations in which we can trust others. Help us to see clearly, and give us the ability to discern. Lord, we wish to be great friends to others, to enter relationships with trust; and at the same time we pray for protection from those who are untrustworthy. Amen.

- *What becomes of the lives of people who are untrustworthy?*

- *What becomes of our lives if we do not trust anyone?*

- *What are the signs and qualities of a trustworthy person?*

Truthfulness

In fulfillment of his own purpose he gave us birth by the word of truth, so that we would become a kind of first fruits of his creatures. **JAMES 1:18**

The truth will set us free

Dear Lord, you have taught us to always be truthful to ourselves and to one another. Grant us the strength and courage to always tell the truth. Help us to overcome those fears or self-interests that prevent us from being truthful. Help us to recognize that being untruthful leads to further trouble and turmoil. Being truthful leads to justice and happiness. May telling the truth be a part of who we are. Amen.

- *Is it always better and beneficial to tell the truth?*

- *How does lying lead to further lies and more trouble?*

- *If you believe lying will help someone, should you lie? Give examples.*

Encourage truth

Lord, it is difficult when people lie to us. It makes us unable to trust them. It destroys our relationships and creates situations that lead to destruction. Help those who find it difficult to tell the truth. May they recognize that it is in telling the truth that they will develop healthy relationships. Help them see that by living a life without lies they will be freed of trouble and guilt, and they will also be freed from the entanglements and the bad reputation lies often create. Amen.

- *Although it can be painful, how can we help others to be truthful?*

- *Why is it that some people find it difficult to be truthful?*

- *Does our society put enough emphasis on being truthful, or does it reward lying?*

Understanding

"While you have the light, believe in the light, so that you may become children of light." JOHN 12:36

Let's wear their shoes

Merciful Lord, we know that you know and understand each of us. You know and understand us because you love us. You know our thoughts before we have them, and you know how we will react before we do. It is with this understanding that you accept us and are able to grant us mercy. Help us to know and appreciate where others are coming from. Help us to be completely open to understanding all people of all religions, cultures, and differing thoughts and opinions. May we acquire the ability to put ourselves in the shoes of others so that we will have a better understanding of who they are and what they do. Amen.

- *What does it mean to put on the shoes of another?*

- *Can we truly know what others are thinking and feeling?*

- *How does putting ourselves in the position of another help us grow as a person?*

We are not the judge

Lord, it is difficult to completely understand people. Sometimes we do not understand why they do and say certain things. It takes a lot of effort and hard work to understand others. Prevent us from becoming lazy, and keep us working hard so that we can make the effort to understand others. We need your help, Lord, to live a life of patience and understanding, free of judging others. Amen.

- *What makes understanding others such hard work?*

- *How do we create a better society through making the extra effort to understand others?*

- *If we avoid judging and work at understanding, will this create stronger friendships?*

Understood (To Be)

O Lord, you are our Father; we are the clay, and you are our potter; we are all the work of your hand. **ISAIAH 64:8**

Teenagers don't get a fair chance

Dear Lord, as teenagers we are often not understood. Some harbor contempt and suspicion against us, and this prevents them from seeing who we truly are. We pray that the world may take on a new view of teenagers; that rather than questioning our abilities and suspecting us, they may support us. We have been blessed with so many gifts and can make great contributions to our community if we are given opportunities and have the confidence of others. Help them see and understand this, Lord. Amen.

- *Are the youth treated fairly by the adult world?*

- *Why do you think some people prejudge or look down on teenagers?*

- *In what ways does society lose when it does not put enough confidence in teenagers?*

We all have something to offer

Dear Jesus, you understood the temperament of your apostle Peter, the ways of Matthew, and the weaknesses of your followers, and yet you accepted them. You saw past their sinfulness and weaknesses and recognized their gifts. We ask that you gift us with that same ability. May we see beyond human weakness and recognize the beauty of others through a greater understanding of them and the human condition. Help us to see greatness in others in spite of their failings. We also ask that you give to others this same gift so that they can see beyond our weaknesses, understand us for who we really are, and appreciate what we have to offer. Amen.

- *Does every person have something constructive to offer, no matter who they are?*

- *What attitudes do we need to adopt to better understand each other?*

- *What does it mean to find strength in weakness?*

Unity

[Nothing] in all creation will be able to separate us from the love of God in Christ Jesus our Lord. **ROMANS 8:39B**

One human family

God of all, through your creation we are all connected as one human family. Help us to experience this wonderful sense of unity. This experience of oneness binds us to your creation in a profound and inspiring way. To see each person as our brother or sister inspires us to work as a community to build a better world. It sets us on a mission that can transform the world, strengthening us to work harder at creating a more peaceful planet. Amen.

- *Do we see the world as one family or as divided?*

- *How would the world be different if we treated each person as our brother or sister?*

- *Did Jesus see the Pharisees and Romans as part of his human family?*

Together, we can accomplish great things

Dear Lord, we know that great things can be achieved when we work together. It is through working together that we will live a life of virtue, practicing tolerance, patience, compassion, courage, and many of the other virtues you have blessed us with. As a community, our values are rooted in the gospel values, and by working together we can create a community based on your message of love. By working together in your presence, we can do much more than by working alone. Amen.

- *Why do we accomplish more when working as a group, rather than alone?*

- *Why do we sometimes shy away from working as a team and prefer to go it alone?*

- *Did Jesus have a team or did he do it alone?*

Wisdom

But the wisdom from above is first pure, then peaceable, gentle, willing to yield, full of mercy and good fruits, without a trace of partiality or hypocrisy. **JAMES 3:17**

Wisdom is valuable

Lord, as we get older, we seem to gain greater wisdom and insight. When we look at our grandparents and other family members who are older, we are often in awe at the things they say, the way they are able to encourage us, and the views they have to offer. Help us to always learn from and be grateful for those in our lives who have wisdom. May we heed their words and give great thought and consideration to all they instill in us. We seek the gift of wisdom and the virtues of patience, prudence, and knowledge to achieve this great gift. We ask this through Jesus our Lord and Savior. Amen.

- *What is a good definition of wisdom? Does having knowledge mean having wisdom?*

- *Who are some of our wisest people?*

- *In what ways do we gain from having wisdom?*

Wisdom offers direction

God of wisdom, what good is it if we have all things but are without wisdom? Without wisdom we run the risk of missing out on many of the fruits life has to offer. We can have all things, and yet if we do not have wisdom we will lose all things. So we pray to you for the gift of wisdom. We pray for this treasure that will bring direction and focus to our lives. We pray for a wisdom that inspires us to give all that we have to others in ways that will bring about your kingdom. Amen.

- *What are some of the fruits of life that wisdom will give us?*

- *Can a person be happy if they do not have wisdom? Discuss.*

- *If you could ask for three character traits, what would they be? Why?*

Wonder

Although you have not seen [Jesus Christ], you love him; and even though you do not see him now, you believe in him and rejoice with an indescribable and glorious joy, for you are receiving the outcome of your faith, the salvation of your souls. **1 PETER 1:8–9**

God is great

Dear Creator, We often look at your creation with wonder and awe. The creation of this earth and beyond is so beautiful that it is sometimes difficult to comprehend. We stand in wonder at your creation—how infinite! And yet every grain of sand is so important. Your creation fills us with feelings that take us beyond ourselves, and yet it draws us into ourselves to see the infinity within. May we hold on to this sense of wonder, propelling us to discover your universe as well as discovering ourselves. Amen.

- *How does it feel to be filled with wonder and awe? Can you imagine a life without it?*

- *What are examples of life experiences that fill us with wonder and awe?*

- *How does this wonder motivate us to discover the galaxies as well as who we are?*

We are wonderful

God of blessings, the gift of your creation and the gift of your love are so wonderful, and yet we often forget this as we travel through each day, entangled in the petty things that bring us down. We pray that we may become more reflective and meditative in our approach to each day, reflecting on the wonder of the universe and the wonder and beauty of ourselves. All of creation, especially each of us, is a marvel and a wonder, beautiful and gifted. We pray, Lord, that we are always open to the beauty and wonder of all of this. Amen.

- *Why are we sometimes more in awe of the universe than of what is within us?*

- *Do we look at others with awe?*

- *What are examples of things that surround us that are awesome works of God's creation?*

Worry

"Therefore I tell you, do not worry about your life, what you will eat or what you will drink, or about your body, what you will wear. Is not life more than food, and the body more than clothing?" MATTHEW 6:25

Lift the worry, Lord

Dear God, we know that all the worry in the world won't change anything. But we are still burdened and overwhelmed with worry.

We pray for peace of mind. Free us from anxiety. Help us, Lord, to take comfort in the knowledge that you are with us throughout our days, and that in times of trouble you are there to carry us. Amen.

■ *Why do we worry so much when we know it doesn't make a difference?*

■ *Does God want us to adopt an attitude of acceptance and surrender?*

■ *What strategies can we use to help us relax and free us from worry?*

We surrender to you, O Lord

Dear Lord, we spend much of our life and energy worrying. Often it is because we are unable to surrender, unable to accept what life gives us. Sometimes it is because we are unable to trust in you. Worry is a heavy burden on us. It takes away our energy and enthusiasm and often prevents us from moving forward. Help us to surrender, Lord, always doing our best, and then handing all things over to you. Amen.

■ *What does the phrase "surrender to God" mean?*

■ *When should we surrender to God, and when should we refuse to surrender?*

■ *Is surrendering considered a weakness or a strength?*

More Resources for Teens!

50 PRAYER SERVICES FOR MIDDLE SCHOOLERS
For Every Season of the Church Year and More
CONNIE CLARK

Using language, ideas, and formats familiar to tweens, these prayers introduce methods like meditation, litanies, intercessions, novenas, and even *lectio divina*. There are noisy prayer celebrations and quiet, contemplative devotions, and prayers to mark seasons and feast days.

144 PAGES | $18.95 | 8 ½" X 11" 9781585958764

LIVING THE BEATITUDES
Reflections, Prayers and Practices for Teens
CONNIE CLARK

Inspired by Pope Francis' call to all young people of the world to "read the Beatitudes," this booklet offers short reflections, simple questions, and activities to help teens and twenty-somethings make the Beatitudes their own.

32 PAGES | $2.95* | 5 ½" X 8 ½" | 9781627850292

BULK PRICING: 1000+...$1.79 • 600-999...$1.89 • 300-599...$1.99
100-299...$2.4 • 91-99...$2.95

SPIRITED LIVES
20 Stories of Saints and their Amazing Gifts
CONNIE CLARK

How do you explain the gifts and fruits of the Holy Spirit? Through the extraordinary lives of people like Matt Talbot, Joan of Arc, Pier Giorgio Frasatti, Josephine Bakhita, Maximilian Kolbe, Thomas More, and many others. Written in a conversational style with room for journaling, this booklet is perfect for teens or anyone preparing for confirmation—and anyone who wonders if it's possible to change the world.

64 PAGES | $6.95 | 5 ½" X 8 ½" | 9781627850933

TO ORDER CALL 1-800-321-0411 | **TWENTY-THIRD PUBLICATIONS**
OR VISIT WWW.TWENTYTHIRDPUBLICATIONS.COM